To

HARRY AND SALLY BERKOVE

MY ABRAHAM AND SARAH

IS THIS BOOK

LOVINGLY DEDICATED

NOE & LEE,
VIRGINIA CITY.

Dan De Quille

DIVES AND LAZARUS

Their Wanderings and Adventures in the Infernal Regions

Edited and Introduced by Lawrence I. Berkove

Ardis, Ann Arbor

Ardis Publishers
2901 Heatherway
Ann Arbor, Michigan 48104

De Quille, Dan, 1829-1898
Dives and Lazarus/Dan De Quille; edited & with an introduction
by Lawrence I. Berkove
p.   cm.
ISBN 0-87501-048-2 (alk . paper)
1. Rich man and Lazarus (Parable)—Fiction.   I. Berkove, Lawrence I.
II. Title.
PS1525.D35D5 1988
813'.4—dc19   87-34491
CIP

Photographs courtesy of The Nevada Historical Society (frontispiece) and
The Bancroft Library (page 54).

Contents

Acknowledgments

This book would not have been possible without the archival resources of the Manuscripts Division of The Bancroft Library of the University of California, Berkeley, and the active and intelligent cooperation of its excellent staff. I have only praise for the resources and staffs of the University of Nevada, Reno and the Nevada Historical Society at Reno. Important and timely assistance was also rendered me by the staffs of the University of Michigan-Dearborn Library and the Southfield, Michigan Public Library.

I am grateful for the expertise donated to me by Prof. H. Don Cameron of the University of Michigan, Ann Arbor, and Prof. Rainer Sell, the University of Michigan-Dearborn. Prof. Sanford Marovitz, Kent State University, made time in his busy schedule to read my manuscript and make a number of valuable recommendations. A friend indeed.

Financial assistance from the University of Michigan-Dearborn Campus Grants and AAAC Research Committees were a major help to me in undertaking my research and preparing my manuscript.

Miss Heidi Kubisek was an ideal student assistant. Her careful and conscientious work saved me much time and effort. I also wish to thank my publisher, Ellendea Proffer, for her encouragement and advice, her kindness, and her forgiving nature.

My family made a major contribution to this book. To this day, I have only a superficial knowledge of how a personal computer works and at no time have I ever been able to read, let alone understand, a single page of directions in the thick and arcane manuals that accompanied my word processing program. My son, Ethan, patiently guided me through their mysteries and to his skill I owe the fact that I was able to use them. I thank him for saving them from the sledgehammer and fire and apologize to him for too frequently using language unbecoming to a father and English teacher. I appreciate the adjustments that Naomi and Daniel uncomplainingly made in their lives because of my work and the many discreet contributions they made to The Cause. Lastly, more than I can say, I thank my lovely and talented wife, Gail, for always being there with her understanding, her judgment, and her love.

Biographical and Critical Introduction to
Dives and Lazarus

Dives and Lazarus[1] is the artistic consummation of an unnoticed apprenticeship of more than 30 years. Although some of Dan De Quille's close friends and relatives knew that he occasionally wrote short stories, they thought of him only as a newspaper man, first and last. Not until his death did anyone even know how long and steadily he had labored at what amounted to his second career: that of a serious writer of fiction. Not until now, with this publication, has anyone even suspected the existence in De Quille of the learning, reflection, and talent that slowly and inconspicuously ripened over the course of his writing career and which finally produced a minor masterpiece in the only full-fledged novella he ever wrote.

The story behind *Dives and Lazarus* begins even before De Quille became a journalist. Oscar Lewis observes that the origins of De Quille's writing career go back a very long way: "Two qualities—a facile pen and a liking for printer's ink—manifested themselves early and predetermined what profession he would eventually follow. As a young man in Iowa he wrote and submitted manuscripts to then popular magazines of the East. During his wanderings about California he contributed pieces to local newspapers . . . "[2] C. Grant Loomis also reports that De Quille had already established a reputation for himself in western literary circles *before* he became a newspaper man, and refers for example to 54 contributions De Quille made to the *Golden Era* alone between November 25, 1860 and August 24, 1862.[3] These are important indications of the general drift toward writing that characterized De Quille from the beginning, but it would be a mistake to infer from this information that because De Quille became a journalist, he was only a journalist.

Writing was the main way De Quille expressed himself, and an eager and insatiable curiosity kept him supplied with facts, ideas, and tales. He stored his retentive memory over the course of his lifetime with personal experiences, information that he got from the people he knew or met, and from his extensive reading of books and periodicals. He was respected for being knowledgeable about his interests (which included Comstock history as well as mining), but the word "learned" would better describe the degree of his understanding of more than one of those interests. His memory supplied both his journalism and his fiction but De Quille increasingly selected different material from his memory for these two modes of writing, and processed the material differently.

It is surprising that there is at present no biography of De Quille, for not only was he an outstanding personage in the California and Nevada of the late nineteenth century, but it is also arguable that he was the best informed writer about the Old West of any of his contemporaries. No other Western writer had such constant close contact, including first-hand experience, with his sources over a more than 40-year span; no other Western writer wrote so continuously, on so many aspects of the West, and in such a variety of genres. It is our good fortune that De Quille was never "just" a journalist, although he was a very good one. In the fiction that he composed almost from the beginning of his writing career, and of which *Dives and Lazarus* is the delightfully surprising culmination, is an incomparable record of the West and a moving reflection on life by one who was profoundly shaped by the West and who was both its devoted amanuensis and its unsuspected artist.

I

The background of the man who wrote *Dives and Lazarus* is worth knowing, for it helps explain why this work was unsuspected as well as unpublished. He was born as William Wright on a farm in Knox County, Ohio, on May 9, 1829. In 1847, when he was 18, his father moved the family to a farm in Iowa near West Liberty, about 25 miles west of Davenport. Shortly thereafter, his father died and left to him much of the responsibility for the farm and the support of his mother and eight younger brothers and sisters.

Five years later, in 1853, William married Carolyn Coleman, moved to a nearby farm of his own, and began a family. The couple had five children in quick succession, two of whom died in infancy.

There is no account of how good Wright was as a farmer but writing even then was a passion with him. According to his daughter, his first "literary work" was done for the country school lyceum. He did not remain in Iowa long enough to establish any reputation, however, as he became caught up by the gold excitement in California and left Iowa in 1857.

This move touches on one of the most mysterious parts of Wright's life: his family life, for he left his family behind and remained away for approximately 36 years. No evidence of estrangement exists; on the contrary, he appears to have always considered himself a family man. He wrote his family frequently and kept up his financial support of it. Over the years, at least one grown daughter resided with him for some time in

Virginia City, and there is evidence that his wife also lived with him for a while. He revisited Iowa once, in 1863, for the better part of a year, but until he returned there to die in his daughter's house, he appears to have spent most of his married life as a bachelor away from the family home.

By the time Wright arrived in California, the mining activity on the coast had abated and prospectors had crossed the Sierra Nevadas to look for gold on their eastern slopes. From numerous references he makes in his subsequent writing, it appears that he prospected and mined for two or three years in the California-Nevada borderland area from Death Valley north to Lake Tahoe and drifted to Virginia City in 1860.[4]

Wright loved mining activity but did not prosper as a miner. Although he did not strike it rich with his pick and shovel, his writing attracted favorable attention. The newly established *Territorial Enterprise* of Virginia City, Nevada Territory, was one of the western periodicals that liked his contributions, and he was attracted to it. In 1861, he gave up mining, joined the *Territorial Enterprise*, and became a full-time journalist. A spirit of whimsy in him suggested a paronomastic pen name: Dan De Quille. He soon made that name famous and was known by it for the rest of his life.

The *Enterprise* was one of the great newspapers of the West. It is remembered, in the West, as the most distinguished of an insufficiently appreciated group of newspapers with the mildly condescending appellation of the Sagebrush School of Journalism.[5] The name refers to the scores of periodicals that were published in Nevada and eastern California in the latter half of the nineteenth century. This location may itself seem, to many contemporary readers, as a disqualification to fame, but when it is remembered that the area was once the site of some of the richest silver and gold mines the world has ever known, and produced wealth which played a major part in financing the Union during the Civil War, and in supporting California and especially San Francisco for decades after the California gold boom declined, then a little imagination can explain why the area attracted men of literary talent as well as miners and financiers. A significant number of the former went on to distinguished careers in scholarship, law, national journalism, state and federal government, and literature. A list from the *Enterprise* alone would include, besides De Quille, such luminaries of their day as Joseph Goodman, Denis McCarthy, C.C. Goodwin, Rollin Daggett, and the most famous of them all, Mark Twain. Less well known, but also influential on a more local level, were Steve Gillis, Jim Townsend, and Alf Doten. Any one of these men would have been valuable assets to any newspaper; all of them worked at one time or another with De Quille on the *Enterprise*.[6]

Joseph T. Goodman and Denis E. McCarthy purchased the *Enterprise* in 1861 and quickly began to acquire the best editors, writers, and printers they could locate. Their bait was simple: high pay, quality reporting, and editorial freedom. According to Rollin M. Daggett, who worked on the paper in its early years and later became its editor-in-chief, they soon made the paper an eight-page daily, larger than any paper then published in San Francisco, and highly prosperous. It "published more matter than almost any journal west of Chicago" to the point where "fifteen to twenty columns of paying advertisements were left out daily for months together" to accommodate the text. It also acquired an international reputation.[7] Undoubtedly, the quantity and authority of its mining reports for the whole Great Basin region, especially the fabulous Comstock lode, created a demand for it in international centers where mining stocks were traded.

De Quille began his work for the *Enterprise* as mining and local editor.[8] In addition to covering news about mining and the region, he also contributed feature articles from time to time about whatever interested him. It was a job that he loved and stayed with for most of the 32 years of his association with the paper. Wells Drury claims that De Quille was convinced that mining news was the "true calling of a first-class newspaper" in the region. "All other matters to him appeared inconsequential and of no material interest."[9] Although Drury mistakes De Quille's professional dedication to mining news for single-mindedness, certainly in his role as mining editor De Quille demonstrated an expertise and integrity that earned him the respect and trust of both the miners and the mine owners of the region. His opinion was sought out and listened to. His reputation undoubtedly played an important part in establishing and maintaining the *Enterprise* as the dominant newspaper in mining circles. Even much later in his life, his articles on mining were solicited and published by a variety of periodicals, including specialized mining journals.[10]

His outstanding reputation as a mining reporter notwithstanding, De Quille's fame, such as it currently is, rests mainly upon the humorous and historical by-products of the work he did as local editor. Writers for the *Enterprise* had to be multi-talented and personally resourceful. The early years of the paper in particular were unconventional and effervescently boisterous ones. One of the best sources of information about them is Mark Twain, who also served on the *Enterprise* and who has left two remarkable mementoes of those years. One is the group of chapters in *Roughing It* (42 to 55) which describes his duties, his training, and his adventures as a reporter in Virginia City. It is impossible to read those chapters without feeling vividly the high spirits of the "flush times" on the Comstock, when a new land was young, when the reporters were young, when life was antic.

Despite its title, Twain's story, "Journalism in Tennessee" (1869), is the other Comstock memento. It reveals, with slight exaggeration, some of the rough-and-ready aspects of journalism on the Comstock. It is not as far-fetched a story as many readers may believe. Comstock society was not as law abiding as we like to think ours is; the press was more uninhibited and vituperative, and fine points of journalistic law and etiquette were more apt than they are today to be settled by fists and even weapons. Wells Drury supplies an enlightening contemporary summary of Comstock journalistic mores: "It was not absolutely necessary for an editor to fight as well as write, but at least he must show a willingness to defend himself in a manly way and stand on his rights, no matter what the result, or else his usefulness in journalism would be impaired to the verge of nothingness. In other words, he might as well walk the grade [leave town], first as last, since his days were likely to be few and full of trouble."[11]

Daggett relates how Goodman and McCarthy once physically attacked a competitor, and how Goodman, on a different occasion, wounded another editor in a duel.[12] Twain himself had to leave the Comstock as the consequence of his injudiciously (and illegally) using the columns of the *Enterprise* to challenge another journalist to a duel after a prolonged and excessively acrimonious exchange of editorial insults. And Joseph Goodman tells a story of how even De Quille, whose reputation for mildness and inoffensiveness had no equal on the Comstock, felt obliged to take a "manly" course of action. He had enraged a "desperado" named Farmer Peel by writing a truthful account of Peel's misdeeds and urging the authorities to punish him. When De Quille subsequently learned that Peel was inquiring after him, he went after Peel and found him at a bar. De Quille sidled up to him, held a stiletto to his throat, and offered to settle any grudges on the spot. Peel backed down and De Quille passed the test of courage.[13]

This sort of life-and-death confrontation was not, however, characteristic of De Quille's activities as local editor. Much more typical were routine reports: social events, fires, arrests and court cases, and also articles on local agriculture. (In the early days especially, agriculture was an important activity around Virginia City.) Sometimes, when news was scarce, De Quille had to be imaginative with what he had. In Chapter 42 of *Roughing It*, Twain tells a delightful story of how he emulated De Quille in developing the news possibilities of a single hay wagon that came into town on a slow day.

De Quille had worked on the *Enterprise* only a few months before Samuel Clemens joined it in the summer of 1862. He and De Quille quickly struck up a friendship. De Quille was a bit older—33 to Twain's 27—and more experienced, but he was very easy to get along with, and he was willing to share what he knew with the younger man in a non-intimidating way, unlike Twain's earlier mentor on the Mississippi River, the pilot Horace Bixby. It is practically the unanimous opinion of all of their mutual Comstock friends that De Quille taught Twain important things about reporting and writing. Twain himself said that "The first big compliment I ever received was that I was 'almost worthy to write in the same column with Dan De Quille. . . .'"[14]

The friendship was to be a fateful one, ultimately, for De Quille, although at first it appears that it was Twain who was most influenced by the other. Like William Wright, Samuel Clemens had shown much more promise with his pen than with his pick. On the strength of some contributions he had made to the paper, he had been offered the position of city editor on the *Enterprise* by its editor-in-chief, Joseph Goodman. Again like William Wright, Samuel Clemens chose a paronomastic pen name for himself, "Josh." And once more like Wright, Clemens had a streak of humor in him which he was delighted to learn was appreciated at the *Enterprise*, particularly when news was scarce and columns had to be filled on short notice.

Clemens arrived at the *Enterprise* just in time to be given a few months of breaking-in experience before De Quille left in December to return to his family for a visit. So solidly had De Quille been accepted into the Comstock by then that a brief spate of editorials from Western newspapers as far away as San Francisco took notice of De Quille's departure. Clemens gave him a friendly farewell in an *Enterprise* article on the day he left, and noted that he had earned a reputation for herculean labors. Tongue in cheek, Clemens observed that this penchant for overwork had gradually undermined De Quille's health somewhat because, in addition to a shortage of regular news, he had also fallen "under a scarcity of pack-trains and hay-wagons. These had been the bulwark of the local column."[15] Among the kindly sentiments and compliments expressed in the other testimonials is one which is unusually specific:

William Wright—better known to his intimate friends and the public as "Dan de Quille"—leaves on the Overland stage, to-day, for his home in the East. Mr. Wright is an old resident of the Territory, and for the past eight months has been connected with the *Enterprise* in the capacity of local editor. In all the walks of life he has won friends, and especially has he endeared himself to his associates in this office. Amid the trying and vexatious duties of journalism his conduct has ever been marked by a quiet, dignified and gentlemanly bearing; and the genuine simplicity and nobleness of his character are such as we have rarely met with. He was as reliable as a fixed law of nature. both [sic] in his opinions and the discharge of his duties. His long experience gave value to his opinion on mines and mining operations, and we fear it will be long before we find another on whose perception and judgment, in this respect, we shall so implicitly rely. Though exceedingly practical in his views, he possessed a keen perception of the humorous, and often made the dullest subject radiant with his genius, while some of his more finished efforts will rank favorably with the best humorous writings of the day. He revisits the East after a long absence, and half of our regret at parting is allayed by the assurance that he will soon return to his adopted home, family and all. We heartily bid him God speed—and if no more inviting field allures him, he will ever find a welcome seat beside us.[16]

De Quille returned to Iowa in December, 1862, by the overland route, via Salt Lake City and Denver, making friends along the way and evoking favorable comment in the columns of local newspapers. But whatever plans he might have had for bringing his family out West with him seem not to have materialized. He returned to the West in August 1863 via New York City and the isthmian route. The Civil War was in full course and the Atlantic part of the trip seems to have been attended by some concern—unrealized—that the ship might be attacked by a Confederate raider. De Quille much later in his life published several memoirs, perhaps partially embellished, about the voyage south and a short visit on the isthmus.[17] He picked up a steamer north and arrived in San Francisco on August 28, 1863. Practically the first thing he learned upon disembarking was that a large part of Virginia City was in flames and riots were sweeping the city. He hurried back to resume his duties and to relieve Clemens, who on September 6 left for San Francisco and a brief vacation.[18]

The friendship between the two men deepened once Clemens returned to Virginia City; they became roommates as well as colleagues. Clemens had changed in some important ways while De Quille was away. For one thing, he had replaced the pen name "Josh" with the one he was to make famous, Mark Twain. Even before De Quille left, Twain's genius was making itself apparent and giving him considerable reputation along the Coast as a skillful writer and accomplished humorist. Edgar Branch notes that at least one perceptive Eastern critic, Fitzhugh Ludlow, singled Twain out in November 1863 as an independent and unique talent,[19] and the influential and famous Artemus Ward urged him early in 1864 to "leave sage-brush obscurity" for wider audiences.[20] A further change, as De Quille significantly points out in one of his memoirs of Twain, was that although Twain continued to develop his humorous techniques, he wrote very few long pieces for the *Enterprise*.[21] And finally, whereas De Quille was universally liked and respected, Twain was not.

In brief, Twain's humor was typically cutting and often made enemies, whereas De Quille's was almost always gentle and good-natured. This generalization, of course, like all other generalizations, has some limitations and some exceptions, but a convenient comparison may illustrate what is intended by it. In October, 1862, Twain wrote his famous hoax about the discovery of a petrified man. The piece is short, and was passed off as a news story. An unusually alert and skeptical reader might have been tipped off by the suspicious subject itself to be on his guard. If he got to the ending without catching on, however, the crude gesture implied by the relationship of the petrified man's spread open hand to his nose would have made the hoax obvious. The humor is clever, but also edged, as the piece was also intended as a satire of a local coroner. Three years later, in 1865, De Quille published a sketch in the *Golden Era* on a similar subject—thus significantly establishing a probable influence of Twain on him—entitled "A Silver Man." De Quille's piece also begins with the discovery of a scientific impossibility, the complete mineralization in silver of a human body, but he then proceeds to make it sound plausible by seeming to substantiate it at considerable length with an abundance of pseudo-scientific and historical detail. The tone is kept serious, the rationalization is specious but clever, and the piece ends up as an elaborate joke, drily witty, ingenious, but with no ulterior purpose beyond entertainment. What began, therefore, as a comparison, ultimately becomes a contrast because Twain and De Quille developed in divergent directions by following the natural bents of their respective temperaments, inclinations which increasingly separated them.

It was not possible in the sixties, without the wisdom of hindsight, to have realized just how important were the temperamental differences of the two men. Although they appeared to be slight at first, they became more pronounced over time and ultimately became distinguishing differences. Edgar Branch has perceptively discussed a number of these fine distinctions in his account of De Quille's influence on Twain. He notes that both writers shared some important social values as well as literary techniques, but concludes that Twain was more daring, or extreme, than De Quille, and sharper in his mockery of his targets.[22] In other words, Branch implies, De Quille had reached a sort of plateau in his development, whereas Twain was still growing and his genius was exploring its capacities. This is accurate as far as it goes, but Branch, whose main subject is Twain, does not examine De Quille in detail once the writers each went their separate ways.

Scholarly comparisons of De Quille and Twain have always, without exception, worked against De Quille, even when De Quille has been viewed sympathetically. There are two reasons for this. One is that, by virtue of the very frame of reference which considers De Quille an influence on Twain, it is understood that Twain became much the greater author; thus the game is loaded against De Quille. By this standard, any contemporary writer who influenced Twain would also come out second best. The second is that little is known about De Quille after Twain left Virginia City. It is generally assumed that after 1876 De Quille dwindled away as a writer, having reached his limit, and henceforth wrote little of interest to literature. This assumption is wrong, on both counts. De Quille's output of fiction greatly increased after 1876. Furthermore, the best of De Quille was yet to come, and it was not to be something that compared with anything Twain had yet written. It was to be a unique work: *Dives and Lazarus*. In 1864, when Twain moved away to greener pastures in California, not even De Quille suspected that he had the novella in him, or even the capacity for such a work. His fiction writing career first had to undergo years of development, which it did in stages.

II

The first stage was his apprentice period, when he began to learn the trade of writing. This was completed by 1864, when Twain left the *Enterprise*. Journalism, humor, tall tales and hoaxes, descriptions of travels, short fictitious anecdotes—the sort of material on which he established his reputation on the *Golden Era* magazine and the *Territorial Enterprise*—were the early products of his pen. It is clear that his skill as a writer came quickly to him, and it is evident from this early work how much he and Twain had in common at that point and why they got along so well.

The second stage was the 12-year period between 1864 and 1876, when he published *The Big Bonanza*, the most significant non-fiction achievement of his life and, hitherto, his last major achievement of which scholars have been aware.

Another specialty of these years was his development of short literary hoaxes he called "quaints." These were humorous, tongue-in-cheek accounts of wildly improbable events that were posed as news items. Today we would call them "put-ons." De Quille's goal in writing them was always the same: to gull unwary readers by his matter-of-fact style and copious use of speciously corroborative detail into believing them true. He first began writing them—"A Silver Man" was one of his earliest —when Mark Twain was still a colleague on the paper, but the most famous of them stem from his second stage.[23]

The interaction between De Quille and Twain had been intense, though short, and De Quille was influenced by Twain more than he realized. Although regular contact between the two atrophied with the departure of Twain, he continued to play a significant role, unintended and partially subliminal, in De Quille's development.

One clue to the nature of this influence is supplied by a long and remarkable letter that De Quille wrote to his sister on January 24, 1875. It reveals that beneath the appearance of gentleness, mild manners, and self-effacing diffidence that both blessed him and cursed him his whole life long, De Quille was uncomfortably aware of his failure to get his fair share of life's rewards. In it, De Quille atypically released a rush of pent-up frustration and anger over his failure to make money and to achieve the recognition he thought due him as a writer.

> Our millionaires, shrewd as they are, are no writers. I could say what they are trying to say, therefore I stand in the light of their champion—but they deliver over their dollars

<blockquote>
with a poor grace and sometimes I have half a notion to show them the terrible damage I could do them in a single paragraph. But too many of my old friends would be hurt. Those who are trying to put stocks down would give thousands to know what I could tell them in three lines, yet they have never thought of it. I could knock the California stock down $100 per share to-morrow by asking a single question. . . .
</blockquote>

Whether or not De Quille really had all this power is now a moot question, but this letter is a revelation of feelings of bitterness and pride not usually ascribed to him.[24]

From frustration over power and money, De Quille then moved to a notice he had just received from a New York paper rejecting his humorous sketch, "Pilot Wylie." He guessed that the editors "were afraid of getting into trouble on account of the real names of Sam Clemens (Mark Twain) Capt. Sam Bowen, and old Wylie being in it." Then, "I don't care the snap of my fingers for Mark Twain nor in what way I make use of his name. . . ." This is such an atypical letter that it is hard to know if he fully meant what he said, especially since he softened this remark two sentences later by accusing the East of being afraid of the West's "off hand and irreverent way of mentioning men of note and standing." But even the most charitable reading of this statement has to acknowledge some conscious resentment and, possibly, envy of Twain.[25]

From here De Quille informed his sister that he was being "pushed and crowded . . . every day" to work on the book that eventually became *The Big Bonanza*. His opinion of the sort of writing he expected to do on it, however, was low.

<blockquote>
All I have to do to make money if all else fails is to turn clown and publish a book. I can get all the money I want. Many men with their pockets overflowing would almost turn them wrongside out for the sake of having a paragraph in the book about themselves, when if I were sick and destitute and not likely to print a book would not give me a single dollar.
</blockquote>

About the only bright spot in the letter was his information that the "Golden Era folks want me to write for their paper. They say they have a little coin to distribute among writers of *note*."[26]

Oscar Lewis interprets this letter as reflecting "a mood of resentment common to many newspaper men in like situations." De Quille, he points out, had over the years seen many men inferior to him in ability rise to positions of wealth and power, and resented the fact that although his reputation as a respected and trusted mining reporter was "an extremely valuable asset" to the *Enterprise*, "yet he remained year after year an overworked newspaper-writer on a salary of sixty dollars a week."[27] Undoubtedly, Lewis is correct as far as he goes. But one of the men who had left De Quille behind was Mark Twain. By 1874 Twain had not only parlayed journalism into national fame but had also published *The Cele-*

brated Jumping Frog of Calaveras County, and Other Sketches (1867), *The Innocents Abroad* (1869), *Roughing It* (1872), and *The Gilded Age* (1873). The rejection of De Quille's "Pilot Wylie," especially for the suspected reason of a lawsuit from an eminent author, a man "of *note* and standing" (emphasis added),[28] had to have made De Quille painfully aware of how far behind his erstwhile colleague he had fallen. The offer from the *Golden Era*, therefore, not only salved his wounded pride but also apparently reinforced his resolve to be an author of "*note.*" That would only have meant, under the circumstances, an author of fiction.

As a matter of fact, De Quille had begun to write stories in the late sixties. The desire to emulate Twain was not the only motive behind this addition to his journalistic repertoire, but an earlier letter to his sister Lou establishes that it was a consideration:

> Mark Twain has been republishing some of his sketches in pamphlet form; 32 pages, price two-bits—"Jumping Frog," etc. He keeps grind [torn] these things over and over a [torn] long as he thinks there is a cent in them. I have his last batch and will send you the pamphlet as soon as I have glanced it over. I never could see much in the "Jumping Frog," yet that yarn was the one which first brought Mark into notice. . . . [29]

Though De Quille confessed bewilderment about the reasons for the success of the "Jumping Frog," it is significant that many of his early stories were local color stories, like the "Jumping Frog." Local color fiction, of course, was an established genre well before Twain and De Quille began writing, and other authors of the West Coast had been writing it. Nevertheless, Twain's example and his success at it must have been a special inducement or spur to De Quille. The fact that dramatic adaptations of *Roughing It* and *The Gilded Age* had been produced in 1873 and 1874[30] also might have been one of the factors behind De Quille's temporary interest, expressed in a January 31, 1875 letter to his sister, in writing a play of his own.

De Quille's 1874 letters back home make constant reference to the stories and sketches he was writing and where they were being published. His fiction was not as good as Twain's but it was good enough to be getting favorable receptions in the East as well as the West. His name was recognized by some New York City editors and they were beginning to solicit him for contributions. De Quille was also extending his literary range; he was trying his hand at different sub-genres in the local color tradition: humor, ghost stories, legends, and his own specialty, the pseudo-historical hoax.

It is clear from his letters of 1874–75 that he was seriously interested in publishing an anthology of his fiction. Just as he was about to move ahead with this project, however, he was suddenly diverted by some very attractive temptations. The Big Bonanza, which Lewis calls "incomparably the richest silver strike in American mining history,"[31] had been discovered in 1873 and the Comstock was just entering upon the biggest—and last—boom in its history. De Quille had been sought out in 1874 by some of the Comstock millionaires to write the story of the mines, possibly as a means of encouraging stock speculation.[32] The prospect of getting backing for a book which would yield him both fame and money was one he did not feel he could ignore, and so as late as April 1875, De Quille vacillated, hoping to be able to work on the new book, which he called *The Big Bonanza*, at the same time he put his anthology of fiction together. This vacillation was ended by the intervention of Mark Twain.

Despite De Quille's ambivalence about him, Twain was one of the friends De Quille sought advice from in an effort to resolve his doubts about which course of action to follow. Twain had no doubts about the matter; he convinced De Quille to have the book published by his own publisher,[33] suggested the prices to be charged and calculated the profits that De Quille could expect, then invited De Quille to come to Hartford and write the book at his house.[34] Twain succeeded in persuading De Quille to concentrate on *The Big Bonanza* and go to work immediately on it. De Quille took temporary leave of the *Enterprise* in May and was in Hartford by June. The manuscript was largely finished by late August, during which time Twain's enthusiasm for the book seems to have cooled. De Quille returned to Virginia City around the beginning of September. The book was published a year later.

The Big Bonanza is an important achievement. Twain's glowing predictions of its success and the pecuniary rewards that De Quille would reap did not come to pass, but the book's reputation is secure; it is the classic contemporary account of the phenomenon of the Comstock, a still delightfully readable blend of history and humor. Without Twain's timely intervention and assistance, the book might never have materialized in the form that we know it, something like a more factual *Roughing It*. But an unfortunate and unintented casualty of its publication was the anthology of fiction De Quille had wanted to compile.

The Big Bonanza was published at just the right time. It could not have been written before 1873, when the Big Bonanza was discovered, and it would not have been a likely project after 1877, when the profitability of the Comstock mines began a rapid and irreversible decline. On October 26, 1876, in fact, a disastrous fire swept across Virginia City, destroying most of it: mine buildings, homes, shops, offices, and the *Enterprise* plant. The fire is described in the last chapter of *The Big Bonanza*, as is the remarkable accomplishment of rebuilding so quickly "that a new town seemed to spring up out of the ground." As far as the town was concerned, however, the rebuilding was a brave but vain attempt. The heyday of Virginia City and the Comstock was over. But De Quille was not to be a casualty of the decline of the Comstock for his literary career moved into a new and exciting phase.

III

The third phase of De Quille's writing career took place between 1876 and the early 1890s. The decline of mining meant that the population of the region began to dwindle. As a consequence, the importance and profitability of the *Territorial Enterprise* diminished to the point that it ceased publication in January 1893. Once this process of decline began, it was certain that De Quille's resentment at being overworked and underpaid on the *Enterprise* was not going to be remedied, and that the newspaper would be even less effective than it had been in the past in furthering his hope of gaining recognition as a serious writer of fiction.

But even before De Quille had begun contemplating publishing an anthology of his fiction, he had stopped depending upon the *Enterprise* as his sole avenue of publication. As far back as the sixties, other periodicals in the West, in other regions of the United States, and even in England, had re-published a number of his "quaints" under the then popular practice of printing "exchanges": news items or feature stories freely available from other papers. He had achieved somewhat of a reputation through this channel, and he soon found that he was being commissioned to write occasional news stories for other papers and being solicited for feature contributions of humor or fiction.

At first these fictional contributions were reprints or revisions of stories he had first published in the *Enterprise*, but as his dissatisfaction with his salary grew, and as it became increasingly clear that the *Enterprise* was in a state of decline, De Quille became more and more aware of the advantages of sending his new feature work to periodicals that would pay him for it. His letters home in the mid seventies are full of references to stories he was revising and publishing elsewhere for supplemental income. It has been generally believed that De Quille declined along with the *Enterprise*, Virginia City, and the Comstock.[35] Nothing could be farther from the truth. On the contrary, De Quille stepped up his freelance activity, varied his style, and found markets elsewhere.

This new burst of literary activity was not completely self-motivated. Some personal problems which had bothered him for about 20 years became critical in this third phase of his writing career. The sad truth is that De Quille's life and his relationship with the *Enterprise* were far rougher and more uneven than has been realized. De Quille's friends (of whom he had many) often characterized his personality in superlatives. He has, even today, the reputation of having been modest, good humored, and even-tempered. Relative to the rough, volatile, and some-

25

times lawless population of the Comstock, De Quille might indeed have seemed exemplary, but we now have important information about his life which reveals a less well-known and ideal side of him.

The Journals of Alfred Doten,[36] the collected diaries of a well-known journalist on the Comstock and a personal friend of De Quille, depict a De Quille that may come as a surprise to many. In Doten's daily records of the late sixties, for example, there are frequent notations to his having "cruised with Dan" or "ran with Dan" as a summation of nightly activities. In the parlance of those times, those phrases meant what "went out on the town" implies to us. It will surprise no one that drinking, frequently heavy drinking, was a major component of Comstock "cruising." If Doten's journals can be believed over their span of more than 30 years' reference to De Quille, De Quille had a problem with liquor. Increasingly, mentions of De Quille's having been drunk the night before are followed by comments that De Quille needed help on the next day to do his work, or that he could not do it at all. By July 8, 1869, De Quille is reported as leaving for California to sober up; by December 24, 1869, he is reported as being in the sixth day of an attack of delirium tremens.

Brawling was another activity frequently associated with "cruising." Doten's entry for April 4, 1867, for example, reports:

> Dan got into a muss while drunk at Wood's Bank Exchange about 4 o'clock this morning in the course of which he called Billy Gregory a "son of a bitch"—Billy struck him with his fist, full on right cheek, laying it open some, and blacking his right eye, swelling his nose, & darkening his left eye a little—I had to localize [serve as local editor] for him this evening & will for 3 or 4 days till he gets once more presentable
> . . . .

While this sort of entry is unusual, it together with the frequent references to drunkenness clearly show that De Quille was not immune to passions or the pressures of his work.

But it was drinking that caused De Quille most of his trouble. It so incapacitated him that even his friend Joseph Goodman, the owner and editor of the *Enterprise*, first warned him that he would be fired from the paper and then fired him, not just once, but several times. Doten's entry of January 27, 1873, notes for instance that "Dan left me and went on the *Enterprise* today, because they wanted him and he has got all right and straight once more—Has been off the Enterprise about 6 months, by reason of dissipation—" Whenever he was laid off, De Quille had to depend upon friends, including Alf Doten (who had become first the editor and then the owner of the nearby Gold Hill *News*) for work or money. This pattern of events also partially explains why De Quille's *Enterprise* salary remained at only $60 a week after 12 years. It explains the entry of January 14, 1873: "Dan De Quille came down to see me and borrow money to pay his room rent, for he is hard up—I lent him $20 and put him to work localizing at once. . . ." And it casts light on the way he used liquor to get relief from problems. On March 1, 1875, for example, only several weeks before De Quille re-established contact with Mark Twain to ask him for advice on book publishing, Doten put this entry in his journal: "Dan De Quille has taken to drinking again the last three or four days after abstaining entirely for the past two years—" Nor did De Quille's visit with Twain and his publication of *The Big Bonanza* break the habit. The late seventies were stressful years for him. After a visit to the County Hospital on February 18, 1877, Doten wrote: "Met Dan De Quille—He has been there about 2 months from drinking and using himself bad, but is nearly ready to leave—"

De Quille seems to have been fired again from the *Enterprise* in 1885 and kept off it for close to two years. Doten's entry of February 26, 1887, reports that De Quille was about to be reinstated at the express order of his friend, wealthy mine-owner John W. Mackay, "1/2 proprietor of the concern." By June, however, De Quille again occasionally had to have his work done by someone else because he was too drunk to do it himself.

Some of De Quille's colleagues with similar problems simply burned out. It is not so remarkable that De Quille was affected by alcoholism, therefore, as it is that he was not defeated by it. It took its toll of his general health but, paradoxically, it caused him to marshall his inner resources and become more independent. In between alcoholic lapses, he drove himself to produce more writing. When he was laid off from the *Enterprise* or otherwise punished by the owners or editors who succeeded Goodman (who sold the paper in 1873), De Quille became more resourceful about contacting friends and acquaintances all over the country for assistance in publishing. Many of them showed their respect or loyalty by responding. One such person, for example, was De Quille's former colleague on the *Enterprise*, Judge C.C. Goodwin, who by the mid eighties was the editor of the Salt Lake City *Daily Tribune.* Goodwin wrote De Quille that he was "sorry to think any concentration of meanness had driven you from the place which you had honored for more than two thirds of an average lifetime . . . " and invited him to "send as you can and we will pay as we can."[37] That particular contact made De Quille a regular and long-time contributor to the *Daily Tribune* on topics as varied as mining reports, political and economic commentary, humor, memoirs, and history. Arthur McEwen, another former journalistic associate on the Comstock who later became an editor on William Randolph Hearst's newly acquired San Francisco *Examiner*, the greatest paper on the West Coast and one of the greatest in the country, also opened up its lucrative pages to De Quille.[38]

By 1885, De Quille's free-lance earnings were at least a significant part of his income and sometimes all of it. He was paid as little as $4 for a slight sketch in a newspaper to as much as $25 for a story,[39] and $20 to $35 a month from the *Daily Tribune*, depending on the number of columns he sent in (stories were extra). De Quille seldom earned what he thought his stories were worth, but by writing a great deal of occasional and topical matter, and sending out revised or "recycled" stories to a wide variety of periodicals, he brought in money from many sources. An August letter to his sister Lou gives us an idea about his finances as well as his activities:

> You ask what papers I am writing for. Well, at present I am writing for the New York "Sun," the New York "Weekly," the Carson [City, NV] "Free Lance," from two to three columns a week for the Salt Lake City *Daily Tribune* . . . and an occasional article for the Virginia [City] Chronicle and one or another of the San Francisco papers. I should have answered your letter sooner, but that I had to write a story for the New York "Weekly." It is entitled "Bendix Biargo" and is in five chapters. The N.Y. Weekly is a story paper. Generally you are obliged to read about six months in it to get to a single marriage; now in my story I have a marriage in every chapter, which I think is a big improvement upon the stories that most of the young ladies are writing. Bob Burdette, Ned Buntline, Josh Billings, among others not unknown to fame, write stories and sketches for the weekly. I wrote my story in one day and two nights, working one night till 3 A.M. and till 2 1/2 A.M. the next. Last Saturday I sent three sketches to the "Sun" and to-day sent my usual contribution to the Salt Lake City "Tribune."[40]

The letter was sent with the enclosure of another story of his that had been recently published.

Even though his stories were of uneven quality, the mere fact that he wrote some of them quickly does not necessarily mean that they were potboilers. De Quille was never at a loss for plots and ideas; he did not have to agonize over what to write. The makings of stories and sketches were practically his daily bread. What he had not encountered himself on his travels or in his personal contacts with the vivid personalities of his time, he heard second-hand. He filled pages of his notebooks with plot summaries and lists of topics that he felt he could turn into narrative. Naturally, most of the stories centered around interesting Western characters or episodes. Some resembled expanded vignettes of the sort Twain used in *Roughing It*. A few stories about blacks use characters that are mildly reminiscent of Uncle Remus, or of Jim in *Huckleberry Finn*.

Years of discipline and experience had given him an impressive facility at extemporaneous composition. He was famous among his colleagues for his ability to sit down and quickly produce a story or article, but he also had a craftsman's concern for anything that he released and he revised stories that he thought worthy of improvement. That his stories were well received and found markets is proof that they had at least a sufficient level of literary quality. Some of them also reflected his personal values although as yet he did not feel strongly enough about any issue to write at length about it.

In the above letter, De Quille compared himself to Burdette, Buntline, and Billings. These writers were entertaining enough but their works are now period pieces and they were no competition to De Quille at his best. Unbeknown even to himself, he was about to find a stimulus that would touch him at his deepest level and evoke qualities, feelings, and talents that he did not realize he had. Before that could happen, De Quille still had to devise a distinctive style of his own, one that was neither reminiscent nor derivative of Mark Twain's.

De Quille was no longer obsessed with emulating Twain but had not forgotten him. Occasional references to Twain appear in De Quille's journalism, and a close reading of the works of this period may detect some influence of a work by Twain every now and then. An example of this might be seen in a minor sketch entitled "Done Cotch Him!" It is an 1885 dialect anecdote about a conversation between two blacks on how one of them lost money in a stock venture. Some comic effect is sought by the contrast between the literal and figurative levels of their conversation.[41] This sketch might reflect a similar episode between Jim and Huck in Chapter 8 of *Huckleberry Finn*, which was published earlier that year. If so, it might be more accurately termed a case of borrowing back from himself, because Walter Blair cites that episode as possibly having been influenced by a passage in *The Big Bonanza*.[42]

It is not clear at this time to what extent the borrowing between De Quille and Twain was a two-way affair. On Twain's side, in addition to *Huckleberry Finn*, parts of "Old Times on the Mississippi" (1875) and the 1891 essay on "Mental Telegraphy" were intriguingly anticipated by earlier De Quille pieces. But it was not Twain who was stunted by the shadow of De Quille, but vice versa. Insofar as De Quille continued to follow Twain's career and use ideas or situations he found in Twain's publications as inspirations for new items of his own, he reinforced within himself a pattern of dependency. Even a little bit of Twainian influence was too much for De Quille; he needed to be totally free of the man who was unwittingly and unintentionally overshadowing him and whose image continued to inhibit his own literary development.

Other areas of his mind and personality not affected by Twain's shadow had never been adversely affected in the first place and continued to grow steadily stronger. One such area was his reading. Reading played an important part in De Quille's writing because it informed a surprising number of his stories and articles. His reading at first "graced" his writing, supplying it with models of style. Increasingly, it supplied him first with learned allusions and then with subject matter. Ultimately, it replaced his own first-hand experiences and the information that he got from others as the most useful areas, for literary purposes, of his memory.

De Quille got an early start on reading. He listed some of his favorite childhood authors in one of his letters to his sister. James Fenimore Cooper was one and Major Jack Downing was another but best of all was Dickens:

I like something in all of Dickens' novels; can hardly say which I prefer, but think David Copperfield and the Posthumous Papers of the Pickwick Club. Just here I desire to tell you something which will delight you. I have a very distinct recollection of sitting with my hands resting upon the knees of our father . . . listening to him as he read aloud "Sketches by Boz," as they came to us week after week in the Old Philadelphia "Atheneum," a literary newspaper.[43]

Dickens exerted a recognizable though long range influence on some of his stories. De Quille speaks, in another letter, of having "had hard work to steer clear of Old Weller," when he created a character who used such pronunciations as "wolatile" and "wiwacious."[44]

In reading the stories and articles that De Quille wrote over his career, especially those of the third phase of his career, it becomes apparent how wide his range of reading was. The example of De Quille is, in fact, applicable to the careers of many other nineteenth-century authors who, like him, read widely and retentively on their own. It is all too easy to overlook how much these authors gained in breadth and depth from their self-education. To his credit as an auto-didact, De Quille selected the best authors and books. It is impossible to present a comprehensive list of his reading but a few names and titles may suggest the scope of the field. The Bible is alluded to frequently in his writing, as are Shakespeare, *Don Quixote*, and the *Arabian Nights*. He also makes learned mention of Ben Jonson, Burton's *Anatomy of Melancholy*, *Robinson Crusoe*, Swift, Goldsmith, Samuel Johnson, Sir Walter Scott, and Carlyle. Substantial references to authors, events, and personalities from classical literature also frequently occur in De Quille's writings. In sum, though his formal education did not include college, his intellectual curiosity and his retentive memory endowed him with an impressive grasp of the classics of literature, both ancient and modern, and his writing reflected it. With *Dives and Lazarus* comes a much fuller realization of how formative that reading was for him.

Another area of study and reflection that increasingly attracted De Quille was religion. Biographical sketches of De Quille typically note that he was descended from Quakers, but if he ever attended any church there is no mention of it. Nevertheless, he gave thought to formal religion. Two letters of 1875 to his sister Lou contain interesting revelations of his religious position. The letter of January 24 is somewhat mystical:

I cannot, my dear sister, tell you what God is like. The persons who tells [sic] that he can tell you what God is like is a liar. I cannot tell you when the world began or when it will end and the persons [sic] who says he can tell you these things is a liar and a knave. As you desire comfort and to know my faith I will give it to you briefly and very imperfectly leaving you to fill in those parts which seem to be lacking. All there is about it is that I believe that my mind will live after my body and will go into whatever place in all the creation a mind, freed from body and earthly nonsense, may desire to visit. It appears to me that all this mind often is mingled as the air and again is separated when mind stands before mind and then passes between the two minds volumes of thought without any trouble about the words or any need of words. The two minds can move away together as two ripples on a lake or may sink and mingle . . . [end of manuscript][45]

The second, written a few months later, is more concise and specific:

About death: take a wide and general view when you will see that it is the general lot. All that are born must die and we may say that we begin to die the moment we are born. If men might live forever except for some unforseen [sic] accident, then we might weep inconsolably when that accident occurred. As it is we feel bad enough without trying to make ourselves full of the aggravations of grief. I fear you trouble yourself too much about the great mystery of the hereafter and the Great First Cause, Creator and Ruler. As I told you some months since, you know as much about Him as any living being can know and to strengthen your faith in there being such a creator and ruler look upon the heavens and the earth and all that is to be seen therein as His work and as evidence that He *is*—exists. I have no faith in Tyndall's doctrine. It is sensational and unsound. It is nothing making something—not only something but every thing. I send you to-day's *Enterprise* in which you will see what Dr. Holland has to say of Tyndall. The lines I have marked contain almost the same words used by me in a letter written to you a month or two ago. He says you know as much of God as can be known to anyone. You see he is to have an article in the November number of *Scribner*; better get and read that.[46] All that is necessary for your happiness is to say that there is a God who created me and who knows what is best for me—if I was once in His hands I am still in His Hands.[47]

If this can be regarded as a valid, though vague, statement of his theology, it will be apparent in *Dives and Lazarus* that it is only a starting point. He gave much thought to theology over the next decades. Newspapers as well as the popular magazines of the late nineteenth century often ran articles on comparative religion, which contrasted positions on heaven, hell, and other theological ideas. De Quille kept scrapbooks and envelopes of topics which interested him, and theology is well represented. He also took an active interest in the religions as well as the ethnic characteristics of the people of the Comstock. A large number of religions were represented on the Comstock. Besides many sects of Christianity there were also Jews, Chinese, and American Indians. De Quille learned from all of them.

Literature and religion came together for him in the area of myths and legends, which he avidly read and collected. In *The Big Bonanza* he made references to ghosts, Paiute Indian spirits, and various creatures of superstition that the Comstockers brought with them from their countries of origin. His later journalism contains substantial sections on folk lore from all over the world.[48] Part of his study of mythology might have been due to its literary and historical significance, but it also appears that, like the writers of the Renaissance, he sometimes looked upon myths and legends as beautiful and even brilliant personifications of the ideas the more sophisticated religions based on the Bible developed abstractly.

One last activity of the third phase of his development was De Quille's whole-hearted endorsement of the free silver movement. His involvement in the movement can be traced in his weekly columns in the Salt Lake City *Daily Tribune*, especially those of the early nineties. It was natural, of course, for him to be in favor of free silver as his region, his people, and he himself were directly affected by silver prices.

It is nevertheless surprising to observe in his journalism the sustained and bitter passion of his relentless attacks on the opponents of free silver. Feeling Nevada and himself threatened, De Quille stopped at nothing, not even demagoguery, in his fierce assaults on his political and economic foes. Many of his columns were strident and abusive. He freely and frequently smeared his targets with favorite epithets like "Shylocks" and "Pharisees," and was given to making exorbitant charges, as in this sentence from the *Daily Tribune* of September 3, 1893: "The ways of the banking Shylocks and other money manipulators are ways of darkness, crookedness and evil, and have been so ever since they got control of the monetary affairs of the Nation twenty years ago." The historic event that he referred to was what he and other free silver advocates called the "Crime of '73," the act of Congress which discontinued coinage of the standard silver dollar and effectively established gold as the only metallic base of value.

The free silver movement stirred De Quille deeply. It was the last great passion of his life. The silver issue was not an eccentric issue or some local, minor squabble. On the contrary, it was a cause which touched the lives of most Americans in the late nineteenth century.

Although a brief summary of so complicated an issue is risky, some generalizations may be ventured. The free silverites wanted the United States to end the monometallic gold standard and begin the free (i.e. unrestricted) coining of silver into dollars at the rate of 16 units of silver to 1 of gold. They believed several major benefits would result. For one, an automatic market would be created for the silver of the Western mines. This would aid the economies of silver mining states by raising the value of silver and restoring the mines to profitability. Next, unlimited silver coinage would bring a flood of dollars into circulation. Money would be more plentiful and cheaper and interest rates would drop. Consumption would go up and farmers and merchants would sell more. One more benefit would be that debts incurred with tight money could be paid off more easily with cheap money. Proponents of the gold standard argued, on the other hand, that inflation would ultimately hurt the country. Creditors would be penalized by being repaid in devalued dollars. Also, because of a world glut of silver it was selling below the 16 to 1 ratio. Were the United States to coin it at that rate, therefore, it would allow itself to be despoiled of its gold supply, for whoever had cheap silver could demand more valuable gold in exchange.

Perhaps more influential in the long run than the abstract and technical complexities of the economics of free silver were popular perceptions that the masses were being taken advantage of by the financial "establishment." A series of depressions and money panics that afflicted America from the 1870s almost to World War I therefore made the cause of free silver a subject of lively partisanship. The hardships caused by the recurrent depressions and money panics had left the citizenry very sensitive to money policy and somewhat resentful of money lenders and big businesses, which seemed to them to feed and grow fat at their expense. It was widely believed by farmers, miners, small businessmen, and workers that the gold standard was responsible for tight money, and that moneyed interests had connived, in the first place, to foist it upon an unsuspecting country and were now opposing the free coinage of silver in order to preserve the profitability of their investments. The country was divided by the issue. Free silver was generally favored by the mining West, the agricultural Midwest and South, and consumers and small businessmen. The gold standard was supported by big business and banking, the financial centers of the East, and by the federal government.

The free silver issue became the catalyst for an emotional as well as political and economic upheaval in De Quille as he visualized with genuine alarm his country divided into opposing camps: the millionaires versus the masses, plutocracy versus democracy, remorseless Shylocks versus the "race of hardy frontiersmen," evil versus good. He conceived that a sinister international conspiracy was behind the monometallic standard. In his *Daily Tribune* column of December 24, 1893, for example, is one of many tirades he directed against England: "The direct effect of the British monetary system is to kill all individual enterprise and independence and drive the masses into servitude."

Believing all he held dear to be at stake in what he perceived to be an unequal battle, De Quille not only fought on the free silver front, but allied himself with extremist Populism. This association brought out the worst in him, eventually drawing him into uncharacteristic anti-Semitism.[49] He also joined the single tax movement. This last cause was the occasion of a remarkable letter De Quille mailed to Twain from England late in 1890. In it, he asked his "old friend" to write a book exposing the evils that resulted from land being private property.[50] The letter is emotional and not well-written. There is no record of a reply, but we know that Twain did not share De Quille's notions about the causes and cure of America's financial problems.

But Twain and other authors did share De Quille's awareness that serious problems existed. The national economic travails at the end of the century of which the silver issue was a visible symbol are reflected in a substantial number of works of American literature. In addition to *Dives and Lazarus*, a partial list would include such items as Mark Twain's *Roughing It* (1872), *The Gilded Age* (1873–74), and *A Connecticut Yankee* (1889); Edward Bellamy's *Looking Backward* (1888), Hamlin Garland's *Main-Travelled Roads* (1891), Stephen Crane's *Maggie: A Girl of the Streets* (1893), William Dean Howells' *A Traveller from Altruria* (1894), Frank Norris's *The Octopus* (1901), Jack London's *Burning Daylight* (1910), and Willa Cather's *My Antonia* (1918) and *A Lost Lady* (1923). The unstable economic climate in America is even part of the background of Henry James's *The Portrait of a Lady* (1880; 1908) and "The Pupil" (1891), which are otherwise set in Europe. Popular novels of the period such as David Ames Wells's *Robinson Crusoe's Money* (1876) and William H. Harvey's *Coin's Financial School* (1895) deal directly, and polemically, with gold and silver as currency.[51]

Though he originally entered the silver controversy only as a journalist, De Quille's deep involvement ultimately affected him unexpectedly. The passion of commitment which had been aroused in him began to integrate with his lifetime of reading and his religious musings. Something new and unforeseen began to develop within him just as the end of his life approached.

IV

The last phase of De Quille's career was short but most significant with regard to his reputation as a serious writer of fiction. It began a year or two before the shutting down of the *Enterprise* in January 1893 and ended when he left Virginia City for good, a few months before his death on March 16, 1898. Some of his most ambitious and talented writing occurred during it. Aside from his journalistic memoirs of the *Enterprise*, Artemus Ward, Twain, and other Comstock personalities, De Quille not only continued to write and revise conventional short stories for publication, but began to compose what was for him a new kind of narrative: long pieces approaching novella length that were deeply influenced by literature, mythology, and religion. The energy that went into these final innovative achievements seems not to have been sufficient for the practical matter of placing them. None of these atypical pieces saw publication although several of them when made available should rank among his best fiction. *Dives and Lazarus* is the longest and most important of these works.[52]

34

Trouble stimulated De Quille. Just as the difficulties caused by his alcoholism spurred him on to become more resourceful and independent, so did the decline of Comstock mining, his consciousness of the demise of an epic era, and the awareness that his own life was near its end drive him to express the reflections that were at last ripening after a lifetime of development. He had outlived the bonanza times but was not content to silently carry to the grave his love of the pioneer and prospector ethic. His journalistic campaign against the forces that were ending the way of life he had known and loved represented his political involvement on behalf of his times. Just when it seemed he could do no more, he began to write *Dives and Lazarus*.

The writing of fiction is a time-honored way of preserving a moment of history beyond its lifespan. Perhaps De Quille sensed this. There is no hard evidence that this was his rationale for the new literary forms of his last phase, but there is no better explanation. Some inner compulsion urged him to write deeply, to express in literary form what he felt most strongly about. He appears to have made some desultory attempts to earn money from these powerful upwellings, but the evidence suggests that the instinct to record them was greater at the end than even the motive of income. Formerly he was supported by both his journalism and his fiction. In these last years, both he and his writing of fiction were supported by his journalism.

Though the character of the *Enterprise* and his relationship to it had changed over time, De Quille maintained an important association with the paper from its early days in 1862 to its closing in 1893. He continued, intermittingly, to earn a salary from his work on it, and he considered it his home base though he had also become a regular correspondent for the *Daily Tribune* and an occasional correspondent for various other periodicals.[53]

De Quille was genuinely sorry to see the paper close because he understood that the closing sealed the end of a historic era. The San Francisco *Examiner* reacted to the closing by featuring in its January 24, 1893 issue five memoirs of the *Enterprise* by men who had worked on it or had been closely associated with it. De Quille, of course, was one of them. He contributed a retrospective tribute entitled "The Story of the *Enterprise*." On March 19, the *Examiner* ran another reminiscence of his, "Salad Days of Mark Twain."[54]

It has been generally assumed that De Quille was a lifelong optimist who kept hoping against hope that new rich silver veins would be discovered and opened so that the Comstock, Virginia City, and the *Enterprise* would flourish again. The *Examiner* articles, plus two more on Twain and Artemus Ward that he published in the July and August 1893 numbers of the *Californian Illustrated Magazine*, are also generally regarded as nostalgic farewells, the last dying embers of a career. These assessments are dubious. Although De Quille would certainly have been gladdened by a miracle which revitalized the region—and he reported very favorably every new mining development on the Comstock—he would have belied his professional reputation as a mining specialist if he had not understood how marginally profitable silver mining had become. As early as October 25, 1885, he observed that unless a new large body of rich ore was found, Comstock stock speculation was "on its last leap." He reported in his *Daily Tribune* article of September 2, 1888 how even the consolidated Comstock mines were shut down three months out of the year, and the higher wages of Comstock miners—$4 a day as compared to $3.50 and even $3 elsewhere in the region—did not compensate for the down time. And in 1892 he noted that stock prices for silver mines hardly varied because there was so little activity to justify speculation. Indeed his *Daily Tribune* articles on behalf of free silver clearly reveal how well he understood the odds against his position.

As for hoping that the *Enterprise* would get another lease on life, he had long since stopped depending on that paper as the sole means of his livelihood and had become practically self-sufficient. Further, whoever carefully reads these "last" four essays on his *Enterprise* years will look in vain to find teary sentiment in them. They are positive but briskly professional memoirs, full of useful—and salable—information. They are not swan songs.

De Quille continued to write for the *Daily Tribune* and to free-lance stories and sketches well into 1897,[55] when he was 68, although his rate of production appears to have slowed down by 1894. An undated article about De Quille from the Carson [City] *Appeal* clearly establishes the level of his activity at least in the years immediately following the closing of the *Enterprise*:

> Since Dan De Quille retired from the *Enterprise* his pen has been busier than ever. There is an immense amount of literary vitality in Dan, and although he is becoming personally something like Don Quixote, he is still weaving his stories and sketches out of his tireless imagination, and his wit is as sprightly and his powers of description as vigorous as ever. One can hardly pick up a paper of any note that some good thing from Dan is not found therein. Dan is no "chestnut" gatherer, but brimming of old with originality. He now writes regularly for the New York *Sun*, New York *Weekly*, Salt Lake City *Daily Tribune*, SACRAMENTO BEE, San Francisco *Maverick*, Carson *Free Lance* and a lot of other papers of which we have forgotten the names. Whenever a paper wants a new story on short notice it telegraphs to Dan, and grabbing a few quires of paper and a pencil he starts at work so as to have the story ready to catch the next mail. How he manages to write so much and keep it up so long and do it all so well, is a mystery to his oldest friends. People have been watching Dan for thirty years, expecting him to give out, but he keeps on running like an artesian well.[56]

De Quille's intellectual vigor remained with him to the end, but his body gave out. When he left Virginia City for the last time on July 14, 1897, he was described by Alf Doten as:

> . . . so terribly broken down with rheumatism and used up generally that he cannot
> live long . . . . Is racked with it from shoulders to knees, back humped up double and
> is merely animated skin and bone, almost helpless—can only walk about the house a
> little, grasping cane with both hands—has not been able to walk down from his
> residence on A st, Va, to C st & back for nearly or quite 2 yrs—Looks to be 90 yrs old,
> yet was 68 on the 9th of May last . . . .

A memoir his daughter wrote reports him as having become so weak about two months before he died that he could no longer hold a pencil to write.[57]

Nevertheless, it was in the last productive years of his life that he wrote *Dives and Lazarus*, the most ambitious work of prose fiction of his long career. The animus of the story toward wealth, but especially gold, is the most general reason for hypothesizing a late date of composition. The debate in Chapter 6 between Dives and Plutus over gold unmistakably puts Dives on the wrong side. When Dives contradicts Plutus after the god praises silver for being "the money of the many," and when he further boasts about his role as a senator in helping demonetize silver in 1873, Dives precipitates an angry sermon from Plutus on the misuse of wealth that ends with the stormy cry, "hence with thee to hell!" De Quille is so obvious at this point that he comes close to giving the story away. The middle name of Dives, "Auriferous," is also a heavy hint that labels him as a villain and, by implication, vilifies the gold standard as well.

The exact date of the composition of *Dives and Lazarus* is not known. Internal evidence—the story's reference to the historic heavy snowfall of January 1890—establishes that it could not have been completed earlier than 1890. External evidence—glancing allusions to the story in his *Daily Tribune* newspaper columns—suggests that the early part of the story was still being worked on as late as 1893.[58] It is unlikely, moreover, that he would have found the time to finish it until his regular duties on the *Enterprise* ended in 1893. Comparison with several other unusually long unpublished stories that he wrote on what appears to be the same paper stock, one of which can be dated to November 1894, further supports a fairly late date of composition or, at least, of revision.

Dives and Lazarus may also reflect a late date of completion in that it is more subdued, certainly more subtle, in its opposition to the gold standard than were De Quille's fiery and fustian barrages in the *Daily Tribune*, especially those of 1893. The novella appears to be a resignation to the probability that the free silver movement would not succeed in the court of public opinion. Setting the action in the afterlife, where judgment and justice are fair and sure, therefore represents not a surrender to the inevitable, but a confident appeal to the Highest Court. This last, passionate devotion of De Quille to a cause evoked from him an elegant representation of his matured religious beliefs, as contrasted to the inchoate ideas that he set down earlier in his letters to his sister.

Dives and Lazarus would be a far shorter and a far less moving and significant novella if it were only a parable about free silver, with eschatological overtones. Somewhere in the course of its composition, De Quille must have come to terms with the realization that he did not have much longer to live, and put much more of himself into the work than just his political and economic stands on free silver. After the misstep in Chapter 6 of preaching too obviously, he de-emphasized the restricted issue of free silver, per se, and gradually refocused the story on the larger and more absorbing reflection on what the soul might expect after death. Here, in an imaginative and unexpected way, De Quille reveals the influence upon him of the greatest books of Western civilization that deal with the subject of the afterlife: the Bible, the *Odyssey*, the *Aeneid*, and *The Divine Comedy*. Were the influence of these books not patent in *Dives and Lazarus*, not even De Quille scholars would have suspected that he had read them, knew them well, and took them so seriously. Like the big bonanza itself, the richest silver lode of De Quille lay hidden until it was discovered by chance.

One last reason in supposing this to be the work of De Quille's final years is that the novella contemplates death and the accounting of a soul for its activities in life. The conventional view of De Quille as simply a humorous journalist is refuted by his extensive and long-time commitment to fiction and especially by this major work of his which reveals him to have had a deep side to his nature, no less real for being seldom seen. As with many another man, adversity brought out the best in De Quille. The years of diligence, frustration, and tribulation can now be seen to have uncovered not just a capacity, but a talent for study and reflection. It would be an exaggeration to call this work autobiographical, but there are more than a few points of similarity between De Quille and Lazarus, the hero of the story.

If these surmises are correct, the question of why *Dives and Lazarus* was not published may now be addressed. Again, the absence of specific information obliges us to speculate, but the most likely explanation is that after he finished the novella he became too sick to revise and rewrite it further and undertake the work necessary to see it through to publication. That he might have sent out the novella to at least one Western editor is implicit in this unaddressed note that was left with the manuscript:

> Very many personages, places and subjects are introduced of which no hint is given in the headings of chapters. I have been careful to say nothing to offend people of any religion. The menagerie contains the whale that swallowed Jonah, Balaam's ass, etc.; the museum the jawbone used by Samson, Moses' rod, etc. These places are outside of the Celestial City in a park. Although Lazarus passes St Peter's gate he does not enter the city of Jehovah itself, owing to an accident which brings him back to earth.

Therefore I have not profaned the Holy City by entering it and describing the things thereof.

The reason why I have thought of sending you the series of sketches of the adventures of Dives and Lazarus for use in your Sunday paper is because of your being strongly on the side of Lazarus—the people—in the fight for silver. No Eastern paper would touch such sketches, but they would please the miners everywhere on the Pacific Coast. I have spoken to some of our miners about the adventures and found they at once caught the idea of "Dives and Lazarus." Properly illustrated the sketches would make a small book that would sell well among miners and silver men—indeed among all opposed to the plutocracy etc.

It is not known for which newspaper the manuscript was intended, and whether or not the manuscript was in fact sent out and returned. The presence of various spelling and grammatical errors in the manuscript shows that it had not received its final proofreading. The giveaway exchange between Dives and Plutus in Chapter 6, the most conspicuous of two or three flaws in the novella, also suggests that De Quille was not through revising it. He had enough strength to complete the most extended and important work of fiction that he ever wrote, but not enough to give it a final polish.

Its imperfections, however, are too few and too minor to keep *Dives and Lazarus* from being a surprising and significant work, an unexpected find which identifies De Quille as a writer worthy of renewed attention. It is an important manifestation of the American West. Given his background as a pioneer and as a man who was shaped by the West even as he helped create it, De Quille is a classic Western author. His descriptions of and responses to the events of his time would have significance even were they less representative and less literary, but *Dives and Lazarus* is a bonanza of literary history. It is also moving as the drama of souls on their way to judgment. It is, last of all, witty and entertaining. Seldom if ever before in modern times had the afterworld been depicted as a place of delights and wonders as well as awesome encounters. Only a writer with erudition and a bold imagination could envisage and populate so vivid and varied an afterworld as De Quille did.[59] *Dives and Lazarus* is an eminently readable novella, planted in time and place but timeless and universal in its themes.

V

Dives and Lazarus is a distinctively American novella made possible by the influence of the familiar literature of Western civilization. First and last, it is an original adventure narrative in the tradition of such classics of the storyteller's art as *Robinson Crusoe*, *The Arabian Nights*, *Don Quixote*, *Gulliver's Travels*, and Bunyan's *Pilgrim's Progress*. Like the myths it

39

incorporates, *Dives and Lazarus* is fast-paced, terse, and rich in incident. But although it can be read simply for enjoyment, some inquiry into its background and origins enhances the experience of it and reveals its sophistication as an allegory.

The range of reading that went into *Dives and Lazarus* is striking. It was no average bookman that was able to call up the variety of famous characters from mythology and literature who people the remarkable underworld of this book. At least as impressive, moreover, as De Quille's familiarity with so many literary sources, was his detailed knowledge of them. Of course there were handbooks and encyclopedias of mythology, some of which De Quille certainly used.[60] They can account for many general allusions, but not for the truly unusual specific information that he also commands. His reading of original sources had to have been extensive.

The most impressive characteristic of De Quille's use of literature, however, is his ability to creatively modify familiar material into something new. What De Quille has produced in *Dives and Lazarus* is not a selected anthology of unassimilated literary items but a fiction of synthesis. Just as Dante, Spenser, and Milton adapted classical mythology to their purposes, so did De Quille invent details and perspectives that enabled him to convert otherwise intractable data into protean material for new fiction. His treatment, for example, in Chapter 5 of Nyx, the goddess of night, and her twin sons, Hypnus and Thanatos, is unconventional at the very least. The details attending the approach of Hecate, in Chapter 7, appear to be invented, as is the reason Lazarus admires her. The use of electric spring guns by the pygmy elves of the rocks against the giant Jotunheimers is obviously an invented detail. And the friendly telegraphic assistance of a "sprite" of the juniper tree, an external notion introduced into the context of Norse legend, shows how De Quille creates new syntheses with elements from different frames of reference.

De Quille's superimposition and blending of mythologies and religions results in an exceptional feat of synthesis. To move smoothly from Greek to Islamic to Norse conceptions of heaven and hell, and from thence to the blended notions of several Christian denominations about the afterworld, required tact in addition to literary skill. It also required a controlling purpose. That purpose was Christian. However varied and entertaining the incidents and personalities that Dives and Lazarus encounter during their adventures in the "world below," both men know that their journey cannot end among these diversions. Even Dives, after he was courted by Mammon in the wondrous rooms of his cave, still regards himself a Christian and dimly appreciates that although it might be pleasant to wander among or dwell in the "paradises" of the pagan Hades, it would be a sort of punishment for a Christian to spend eternity in them instead of the Christian heaven.

Like so many of the other figures in *Dives and Lazarus*, the two main characters are new creations synthesized from original sources. Dives and Lazarus are constituted from both the New Testament and late nineteenth-century America. As Americans, they represent the opposite extremes De Quille described in his *Daily Tribune* attacks: the millionaires and the masses. Lazarus is one of the many who spends his life in mining for precious ores but only makes a bare living at it. Dives is one of the few who accumulates the scarce gold and profits by making it scarcer. Lazarus is learned, unassuming, and constant. Dives is a pompous vulgarian who is easily intimidated and becomes servile when threatened. Lazarus shares the little he had with any who were needy; Dives cheats even his business partner. Lazarus lives his simple but sincere faith and is fully committed to it; Dives lives only to benefit himself, and presumes he can buy his way even into Heaven. The substantial donations he makes to an eclectic variety of churches and causes reflects not a charitable disposition but a basic lack of faith. They are his way of reducing a risk by hedging his commitment; if one donation yields him no benefits in the hereafter perhaps one of the others will.

The financial and spiritual conditions of Dives and Lazarus originate in *Luke* 16:19–31, the parable of the rich man who went to Hell and the beggar Lazarus who was eventually received in Abraham's bosom. The dictionary derives the name "Dives" from Middle English and, before it, from the Latin word for rich or costly. Although the rich man in the parable is not named, "Dives" seems to have a long tradition of serving as his name. The scant information supplied by *Luke* is considerably augmented by De Quille so that his Dives receives additional first and middle tag names, Magnificus Auriferous, and a history as a sinfully rich American senator. But Dives is not left as a mere stereotype.

Through a number of satiric touches, De Quille creates a convincing character for Dives appropriate to his condition in life and to his destination. We are not asked to take it on faith that Dives is a shallow hypocrite; we see him in action. Dives's attitudes towards the Chinese, for example, expose the disparity between his real and apparent motives. His pretense about importing Chinese laborers so that they could be converted is cynically devised to appeal to the American missionary impulse. Nor is he really concerned about good relations with China. His real motive in both cases is financial; Chinese labor is cheap. Ironically, of course, Dives is wrong to consider himself a true Christian. He presumes himself one of the elect because he was born and raised in white America, and is rich. His fundamental materialism, however, is exposed when awareness that "the true religion is spreading" into Africa and China leads him to speculate that the real estate outside the Celestial City is "valuable" because the City may expand. He further assumes that the Africans will inhabit "quarters" in an outlying district and the Chinese will have a Chinatown in a suburb; presumably whites will inhabit the best neighborhoods in the City itself. All of his life, Dives served Mammon; he has dreadfully underestimated the nature of Christian belief and its consequent obligations to God and one's fellow man.[61]

In contrast, the character of Lysander P. Lazarus is understatedly moral. The name "Lysander" may recall the famous Spartan warrior who, though ambitious and full of faults, was nevertheless free of greed and lived and died poor. Lazarus also appears in *John* 11–12 as the name of the man whom Jesus raised from the dead. Although two different men with the name of Lazarus appear to have been depicted in *Luke* and *John*, they have often been treated as one and the same. We do not know whether or not De Quille was aware of the difference, only that he followed the latter approach.

Lazarus was more of a challenge for De Quille than Dives was, because the New Testament says much more about Lazarus than about Dives. De Quille had practically a clear track as to how he depicted the character of Dives, but with Lazarus he had to decide to change or not use certain details. For example, his Lazarus is a miner instead of the beggar in *Luke*, and no use is made of Mary and Martha, the sisters of Lazarus in *John*. More importantly, Jesus does not appear on the scene to perform the miracle of resurrection, as is the case in *John*. Instead of detailing all the alterations and omissions, suffice it to say that De Quille retained only the biblical plot situations of a man raised from the dead and that of a poor man whose virtuous life had earned him Heaven.

A surprising and humanizing change of character occurs in Lazarus in Chapter 17, as St. Peter questions him before the Heavenly Gate. Up to that point, Lazarus has always been deferential to Dives, and almost too solemn and respectful before everyone else. Most of the humor that has hitherto occurred in the novella is satirical, generated by Dives's ridiculousness. Given a hint of encouragement from St. Peter, however, Lazarus grows confident and wittily engages the saint in repartee, daringly reminding him of *his* shortcomings. This is true Comstock humor, unexpected, improbable, familiarly impertinent. With the sudden emergence of this new Lazarus, De Quille entertains us one more time with his favorite technique of creatively embellishing some history or facts with fictional additions. More seriously, at the same time, he makes the point that the opposite of a Dives is not merely someone without faults.

Less obviously, the allegorical dimension of the novella enabled De Quille to treat with wise silence the whole issue of how and why Lazarus was resurrected. Almost anything he said on this point would have sounded like preaching. In *John*, Jesus performed the miracle of resurrecting Lazarus in order to convince people to believe in him. De Quille knew this, as did his contemporaries. The raising of Lysander P.

Lazarus from the dead would have been every bit as much of a miracle as that narrated in *John*, and only Jesus could have performed it. This point is not made explicit in the story but the logic of the biblical parallel implies it. *Dives and Lazarus*, therefore, subtly understates an affirmation of Christianity and its values. Insofar as Lazarus is saved and Dives is damned, their respective lifestyles also receive justification and condemnation, and the judge can only be Jesus.

Although the allegorical content of *Dives and Lazarus* reflects the New Testament and American history, its structure follows *The Divine Comedy*. And *Dives and Lazarus* is a comedy in the same classical sense that Dante's poem is: the soul's struggle with life ends in victory. De Quille does not follow Dante in great detail, but he makes fundamental use of the general idea of the journey of a soul through the infernal regions and some intermediate states into Paradise. Other similarities are readily apparent: the use of light symbolism, for example, and the presence in the underworld of such characters as Chiron and Plutus. But even these similarities are limited and often handled in a different way. Plutus is again a good example. Dante treats him as a frightening demon in Hell from whom Virgil has to afford protection, whereas De Quille depicts him in Hades as a blind boy, and regards him as a moral and beneficent deity whose good intentions for humanity are symbolized by the cornucopia he carries.

The distinction between Hades and Hell is not original with De Quille but his use of it in a Dantean context is. Dante's severe theology was not De Quille's, who felt as free as Dante had to create an afterworld that conformed to his own preferences. Accordingly, De Quille's afterworld has some cheerful features totally absent in Dante's. This fresh conception of what may lie between death and final judgment is indeed one of the features of *Dives and Lazarus*. Not only are the *Odyssey* and the *Aeneid* tapped for contributions to this new hereafter, but so are mythology and literature.[62] No part of *Dives and Lazarus*, in fact, is more delightful than what appears to be De Quille's original contribution to the literature of the hereafter, the Limbo of Myth and Fiction, depicted in Chapters 10 and 11.

Just as Dante advantaged himself of the cultural legacy he inherited from the past, so too did De Quille. And just as Dante did not hesitate to pass judgment on the events of his own time and on his fellow countrymen, neither did De Quille. From this perspective, the assignment of Dives to Hell is thoroughly Dantean.

Although *Dives and Lazarus* has many influences playing upon it, the genius that assimilated a lifetime of experience and reading, reflected upon it, and refined it with wit, grace, and charm was strictly De Quille's. How easy it would have been for him, not far from his own death, to have become serious and ponderous in his contemplation of the inevitable. Yet on almost every page, the dialogue or description reveals deft incongruities that sparkle with sly wit. De Quille's balancing of moods, his low-key satire, his subtle development of character, his invention, the way he simultaneously advances both light and serious themes, and the rising note of humble optimism on which he ends his novella reveal De Quille, at last, independent of Mark Twain and a comic master. That he achieved an artistic level of originality in his own time and in his own way justifies the confidence in him always maintained by his fellow Comstockers. The journey to *Dives and Lazarus* was a long and arduous one for De Quille, but it ended successfully in a *Divine Comedy* that belongs to America.

Notes

1. The manuscript of *Dives and Lazarus* is in the William Wright Papers (File P-G 246) of The Bancroft Library, the University of California-Berkeley. I wish to thank The Bancroft Library for its permission to publish the work.

2. Oscar Lewis,"Introduction," *The Big Bonanza*, by Dan De Quille (New York: Crowell, 1947), viii.

3. C. Grant Loomis, "The Tall Tales of Dan De Quille," *California Folklore Quarterly* 5 (Jan. 1946), 28.

4. De Quille recalled that Saturday, June 9, 1860, was the date of his arrival in Virginia City in his article, "Our Land and People," Salt Lake City *Daily Tribune*, Sept. 9, 1888.

5. The origin of the term, "Sagebrush School of Journalism," is unknown, but it received an important recognition when Ella Sterling Cummins used it in her valuable overview of nineteenth-century California authors and literature, *The Story of the Files* (San Francisco: n.p. 1893), 102–118.

6. For biographical sketches of most of these men, see the collection of reminiscences of the *Enterprise* by its contemporaries and former employees that Oscar Lewis edited and introduced, *The Life and Times of the* Territorial Enterprise (Ashland: Lewis Osborne, 1971).

7. Rollin M. Daggett, "*Enterprise* Men and Events," *The Life and Times of the* Territorial Enterprise, 13–14.

8. Dan de [sic] Quille, "The Story of the *Enterprise*," *The Life and Times of the* Territorial Enterprise, 8.

9. Wells Drury, *An Editor on the Comstock Lode* (Reno: U of Nevada P, 1984), 211.

10. *The Mining Industry and Tradesman* and *The Engineering and Mining Journal*, for example, occasionally ran both factual and anecdotal articles by De Quille.

11. Drury, 169.

12. Daggett, 15–16.

13. Joseph Goodman, *Heroes, Badmen and Honest Miners: Joe Goodman's Tales of the Comstock Lode*, intro. Philip I. Earl (Reno: Great Basin P, 1977), 33–36.

14. Quoted in Lewis, *The Big Bonanza*, xvi.

15. [Mark Twain], "The Illustrious Departed," quoted in *Early Tales & Sketches, 1 (1851–64)*, ed. Edgar M. Branch, Robert H. Hirst, and Harriet E. Smith (Berkeley: U of California P, 1979), 171–74.

16. Unsigned, undated, and unidentified editorial in a scrapbook in the William Wright Papers. Published courtesy of The Bancroft Library.

17. See "Isthmian Sports," San Francisco *Examiner*, February 5, 1888, and "The Island of Navassa," Salt Lake City *Daily Tribune*, Oct. 27, 1889.

18. De Quille's account of his dramatic return to Virginia City can be found in his article, "Reporting with Mark Twain," *Californian Illustrated Magazine* 4 (Aug. 1893), 170–71.

19. Fitzhugh Ludlow, "A Good-Bye Article," *Golden Era* 11 (November 22, 1863): 4. Quoted in *Early Tales & Sketches*, 23.

20. Quoted in *Early Tales & Sketches*, 23.

21. De Quille, "Reporting with Mark Twain," 176.

22. Edgar M. Branch, *The Literary Apprenticeship of Mark Twain* (New York: Russell & Russell, 1966), 105–9.

23. The best collection of De Quille's quaints currently available is C. Grant Loomis's "The Tall Tales of Dan De Quille," *California Folklore Quarterly* 5 (Jan. 1946), 26–71.

24. De Quille was universally regarded by those who knew him as the epitome of sweetness of disposition. His editor, Joseph Goodman, said of him: "Nothing can ruffle his temper. He is as alien to anger and strife as a lamb. If there were a divining rod that had the power to point out the most upright, inoffensive, and blameless man living . . . it would settle upon Dan De Quille" (Goodman, 33). Another contemporary, Wells Drury, reminisced that "[t]hough Dan never reaped the full fruit of hopes which he secretly cherished, he was not embittered. Few knew the nobleness of soul, the absolute integrity, and the generous nature that dwelt under the modest demeanor that was so natural to Dan De Quille" (Drury, 217). The unqualified and superlative character of these testimonials is somewhat surprising in the light of what Alf Doten reports below, but even he wrote an unqualified eulogy when De Quille died.

25. For a fuller discussion of the significance of "Pilot Wylie" to the relationship between De Quille and Twain, see Lawrence I. Berkove, "Dan De Quille and 'Old Times on the Mississippi,'" *Mark Twain Journal* 24:2 (Fall 1986).

26. William Wright to Lou, Virginia City, January 24, 1875, in the William Wright Papers collection. Published courtesy of The Bancroft Library. The rambling, self-pitying, and extravagant character of this letter suggests that it might have been written under the influence of alcohol.

27. Lewis, xiii-xiv.

28. This phrase is used elsewhere in the letter of January 24, 1875, to categorize Twain. The letter continues: "Here we don't care a d-n . . . whether a man is worth $5 or $5,000,000, we speak of him as we find him." Allowing for exaggeration, De Quille here appears to be, implicitly, further categorizing Twain as rich and himself as poor. "Note" may therefore have the meaning of wealth (the possession of banknotes) as well as fame.

29. De Quille to "Dear sister" [Lou?], Virginia City, June 14, 1874. Published courtesy of The Bancroft Library.

30. By late April 1874, the dramatization of *The Gilded Age* had reached San Francisco and was written up in the papers. See Thomas Schirer, *Mark Twain and the Theatre* (Nürnberg: Verlag Hans Carl, 1984), 41.

31. Lewis, xiii.

32. Lewis, xiii.

33. It was in the March 25, 1875 letter that Twain sent to his publisher, Elisha Bliss, urging him to consider De Quille's book on "the big bonanza," that Twain gave De Quille his famous recommendation: "The first big compliment I ever received was that I was 'almost worthy to write in the same column with Dan De Quille.'" Quoted in Lewis, xvi.

34. The fascinating but complicated account of exactly what Twain said and did to persuade De Quille can be found in Lewis, xv-xxiv.

35. The only exceptions are James J. Rawls, whose *Dan De Quille of the Big Bonanza* (San Francisco: Book Club of California, 1980) reprints some later writings of De Quille, and Lawrence I. Berkove, "The Literary Journalism of Dan De Quille," *Nevada Historical Society Quarterly* 28:4 (Winter 1985), 249–61.

36. *The Journals of Alfred Doten: 1849–1903*, 3 vols. ed. Walter Van Tilburg Clark (Reno: U of Nevada P, 1973).

37. C.C. Goodwin to Dan De Quille, Salt Lake City, February 23, 1885, in the William Wright Papers. Published courtesy of The Bancroft Library.

38. See Berkove, "Literary Journalism," 255–60.

39. The famous biographical sketch of "Snow-shoe Thompson" brought $25 from the *Overland Monthly*, plus an apologetic letter from the editor for not being able to offer more. Letter, dated Sept. 11, 1886, in the Special Collections Department of the University of Nevada—Reno Library. By way of comparison, more than a decade later the *Overland Monthly* paid Jack London only $5 for his short story, "To the Man on the Trail," and London earned only $5 to $7.50 apiece for some of his best Klondike stories. Twain, on the other hand, was one of the most highly paid writers in America. Even in 1875, he was paid $20 *a page* for some of his contributions to the *Atlantic Monthly*.

40. William Wright to "Sister Lou," Virginia City, August 31, 1885, in the William Wright Papers. Published courtesy of The Bancroft Library.

41. "Done Cotch Him!" was published in the *Wasp* on November 14, 1885. For a brief discussion of the story see Berkove, "Literary Journalism," 254.

42. Walter Blair, *Mark Twain & Huck Finn* (Berkeley: U of California P, 1962), 123–24.

43. William Wright to "Dear sister" [Lou?], Virginia City, June 14, 1874, in the William Wright Papers. Published courtesy of The Bancroft Library.

44. William Wright to "Dear sister" [Lou?], Virginia City, August 23, 1874, in the William Wright Papers. Published courtesy of The Bancroft Library.

45. William Wright to "Dear Lou," Virginia City, January 24, 1875, in the William Wright Papers. Published courtesy of The Bancroft Library.

46. See "Topics of the Time: Mr. Tyndall's Address," *Scribner's Monthly* 9 (Nov. 1874), 114–15. This was an unsigned critique by the editor Josiah Gilbert Holland of a "personal confession" of creed by the well-known English scientist John Tyndall. Holland was extremely critical of Tyndall's radical materialism, the belief that everything in the universe, including God, Nature, and Mind, was not spiritual in origin but stemmed from properties of matter. Holland argued that "there are limits to thought. . . . Because Mr. Tyndall cannot find God, is there, therefore, no God?"

47. William Wright to "Dear sister" [Lou?], Virginia City, October 25, 1874, in William Wright Papers. Published courtesy of The Bancroft Library.

48. De Quille's *Daily Tribune* column of July 19, 1885, for example, discusses mine ghosts, including the Getuli and Cobali which are mentioned in *Dives and Lazarus*.

49. Under the influence of extreme Populism, De Quille's criticisms turned to ranting demagoguery. Milton Friedman and Anna J. Schwartz, in a brief survey of Populist and silverite literature, report that Wall Street, England, and Jewish bankers were often linked as plutocratic conspirators, and quote C. Vann Woodward's observation that some Populist agitators "'bore down with peculiar viciousness on the Semitic symbol.'" (*A Monetary History of the United States: 1867–1960* (Princeton: Princeton U Press, 1963), 115.) These comments describe the pattern that De Quille ultimately followed. I say "ultimately," because he refrained from overt prejudice until 1893. Although even his early attacks on the gold standard constantly denounced an economic "rule" of the "Pharisees" and the machinations of "Shylocks" after a pound of flesh, and used other inflammatory Populist rhetoric, he seemed at first to use these terms only metaphorically and not to have intended them literally, anti-Semitically. On the contrary, he published in the July 7, 1889 *Daily Tribune* a long, carefully constructed, and noteworthy essay entitled "America the True Canaan" which is extremely positive toward Jews and appears to represent his dissociation from the anti-Semitic excesses of Populism. This friendly attitude appears again in a brief note as late as August 21, 1892. Something in 1893, possibly the severe economic depression that began then and practically put an end to silver mining, seems to have driven him over the edge, for his usually discursive columns abruptly became single-issue diatribes. An ugly and bitter malice replaced his typical benevolence, and several of his columns make explicitly anti-Semitic comments. For the text of "America the True Canaan" and a further discussion of his anti-Semitism, see Lawrence I. Berkove, "Free Silver and Jews: The Change in Dan De Quille," in a forthcoming issue of *American Jewish Archives*.

50. William C. Wright to Mark Twain, Bournemouth, England, October 28, 1890. In the Mark Twain Papers, The Bancroft Library.

51. See William Benn Michaels's *The Gold Standard and the Logic of Naturalism* (Berkeley: U of California P, 1987) for fuller discussions of how literature of the period reflects the controversy over the gold standard, as well as other economic issues.

52. For an example of one of the new long short stories, see Berkove's edition of De Quille's Indian legend, "Pahnenit, Prince of the Land of Lakes," in a forthcoming issue of the *Nevada Historical Society Quarterly*.

53. As late as October 28, 1897, James Gordon Bennett of the New York *Herald* wrote De Quille and requested that he send him some 200-word messages on the pre-election political situation in Nevada. De Quille was no longer an active journalist and had retired to Iowa at this time, but the request reflects the range of De Quille's reputation. Letter in the William Wright Papers, The Bancroft Library.

54. All six of these memoirs have been collected by Oscar Lewis and republished as *The Life and Times of the* Territorial Enterprise.

55. A letter from Wells Drury in San Francisco, dated June 25, 1897, responds to a recent request from De Quille for assistance in selling his stories. In the William Wright Papers, The Bancroft Library.

56. An undated newspaper clipping in the William Wright Papers, The Bancroft Library. Internal and circumstantial evidence suggests that it was written by Sam Davis, the editor of the Carson *Morning Appeal* and a friend and admirer of De Quille.

57. Unpublished manuscript in the William Wright Papers. Published courtesy of The Bancroft Library.

58. A headline in his *Daily Tribune* column of March 22, 1891, reads "A Bright Outlook Again in the Land of Lazarus." No further use is made of the allusion in the column, however. It is possible, as De Quille states in the unaddressed letter in the novella manuscript (see pp. 38–9), that he had been telling some people about the adventures of Lazarus and that they understood this reference. Similarly, the column of April 12, 1891, uses headlines that come from the early part of the novella but which are left undeveloped and unexplained in the body of the following text: "Down Through That Yawning Gulf,/the Grave, to the Sunless Shore" and "Grippe Making Business Lively for That 'Ferryman, Old and Dread'. . . ." The column of Sept. 10, 1893 concludes with an allusion to punishment in the Fiddler's Green part of Hades.

59. Some idea of the particular richness of *Dives and Lazarus* can be glimpsed by comparing it to two contemporary works that have points of similarity with it. Robert Browning's poem, "An Epistle . . . of Karshish" (1855), is an account by an Arab physician of Lazarus after he was raised from the dead, but the letter focuses on how out of step he is back in this world rather than on what he experienced after death. Mark Twain's *Captain Stormfield's Visit to Heaven* (1908), like many other literary works, has some unconventional things to say about Heaven, but deals only briefly with the trip there.

60. Among his notes on *Dives and Lazarus* is one reminding himself to check on "Diana sweeps by" in the Greek Mythology section of *Chambers's Encyclopedia*.

61. De Quille got along well with the Chinese for most of his career. He reported on them in a friendly manner, and even composed a short work of fiction clearly based on a Chinese legend. It is distressing, therefore, to read in his *Daily Tribune* column of June 18, 1893 his support of the Chinese Exclusion law because "[t]here is between the two races an irreconcilable antagonism." He concludes: "The plutocracy of the country may favor the introduction of Chinese, but the laboring classes will sooner or later rise and slaughter them wholesale if they are permitted to come." This justification of violence is extremely unlike De Quille, but it is in keeping with such other atypical stands of 1893 as his anti-Semitic remarks. Prejudices which De Quille either rejected or successfully suppressed during the rest of his life appeared in this year, possibly because of the stresses of the financial depression and his particular bitterness at seeing the silver mining industry coming to an

end. In any case, the story not only criticizes Dives for importing Chinese as cheap labor but also for thinking himself superior to them in God's eyes. Insofar as the story rejects Dives's racism on Christian grounds—a position in keeping with De Quille's characteristic and long-standing tolerance—this part of the novella would have to have been composed either before 1893 or such time afterwards as when De Quille returned to his normal attitudes.

62. Although they are not primarily concerned with conceptions of the afterworld, Hawthorne's "A Virtuoso's Collection" (1842) and "The Hall of Fantasy" (1843) have enough points of resemblance to *Dives and Lazarus* to merit special attention as possible sources of inspiration to De Quille. Another Hawthorne story, "The Celestial Railroad" (1843), may also be echoed in the novella.

Introductory: The Death of Lazarus.

It was with much surprise and sincere sorrow that all old-time residents of the Comstock heard the news of Lysander P. Lazarus having dropped dead in front of his place of residence. He was standing at the gate in front of his bachelor abode, chatting with a neighbor, when he suddenly fell lifeless to the ground. The alarmed neighbor, and two or three passing citizens, took up the body of the poor man, whom they supposed to have fallen in a fit, and carrying it into his cottage placed it in the bed, when the nearest doctor was brought.

"Not of much use, gentlemen, to try to do anything," said the doctor, as soon as he had glanced at the pale face of the prostrate man; "heart disease is fearfully prevalent of late years in all parts of the world, and that was undoubtedly the trouble here."

After a few minutes' effort at resuscitation with the ordinary restoratives at hand, the doctor said it was, as he had supposed from the first, a case of "heart failure," and the man was undoubtedly dead.

As there were seen no signs of life the body was prepared for burial and placed in a coffin. This was about the middle of January (1890), when prevailed the severest storms and heaviest falls of snow ever known in Virginia City.[1] It was impossible to reach the cemeteries lying north of the city on account of the huge banks of snow that blocked the way. At this time the bodies of several citizens who had fallen victims to *la grippe*[2] were placed in the vaults of the undertakers and there kept for over a week, until the furious snow storm which prevailed had subsided.

The friends of Mr. Lazarus—principally members of the Society of Pacific Coast Pioneers—decided that the body of their brother "Argonaut" should remain in his own house; and that by turns they would watch over it day and night until the funeral could take place.

All had been surprised when told of the sudden death of Mr. Lazarus, and expressions of regret were everywhere heard, but the surprise was still greater to hear at the end of about thirty-six hours that our old friend had revived and was in a fair way to fully recover. Then for a time there was a perfect furor of excitement. Guards had to be placed at the house to keep back the rush.

A full account of the "coming to life" of Mr. Lazarus was given in all the papers of the city at the time; therefore I shall here merely give a brief statement of the facts of the case.

After lying in a death-like trance for nearly thirty-eight hours, counting from the time he fell down at his gate, Mr. Lazarus had suddenly returned to life and the full possession of his senses. As may well be imagined the revival of the supposed corpse was a thing that rather startled those on watch in the house. The coffined body was resting in a small bed-room off the parlor, and in the latter the watchers, four in number—enough for a comfortable game of "Old Sledge"—were seated, with a few "creature comforts" standing uncorked within easy reach. Colonel Bob had just lifted up his voice in exultation over the pleasing circumstances of his having captured Captain Jim's jack, when all were startled at hearing the voice of Lazarus, who was supposed by all to be at the moment safely reposing in Abraham's bosom.

"Are you here, Colonel Bob?" called the voice.

The faces of the four card-players became white as marble in a moment, and as they sat silent with bulging eyes each man who had even a sprig of hair on his head felt it begin to bristle.

Again the voice of Lazarus called: "Are you here, Colonel Bob?"

"He wants you, Colonel," said the others.

"He probably wants us all," said the Colonel.

"He mentioned no one but you," said the others.

Pulling himself together, Colonel Bob had the courage to answer: "Yes, Lysander, I am here. Are you alive?"

"Yes, alive, but jammed in a crevice in a big iceberg and almost frozen. If you can help me out I hope you will come here at once."

"By the Lord, boys," cried the Colonel, "Lysander has come to life! Bring the light, quick!" and the Colonel at once made a dash for the bed-room.

Mr. Lazarus was found sitting up in his coffin and for a time gazed about, seemingly too much bewildered to speak.

The four watchers were all men who had much experience as nurses in the mountain camps of California in the "days of forty-nine," and they soon had their revived friend in bed, where they administered such stimulants and nourishment as his case required.

Mr. Lazarus so rapidly recovered his wits that he soon seemed as well as ever in mind. He was then told what had befallen him and on his part said that feeling very cold he thought he had fallen into a great crevice in an iceberg and was there wedged fast. Hearing the Colonel's voice apparently near at hand, he had called to him in the hope of being hauled out of his uncomfortable lodging place.

"The case is just this," said the Colonel, "he has an indistinct recollection of falling; that was when he fell at the gate, and then he was dead in both body and mind until he came out of his trance just now, and being cold imagined that on falling he had landed in a cleft in an iceberg. He connects these two circumstances, all the rest is blank," and the Colonel had settled the matter so satisfactorily that all present nodded approval.

In two or three days Mr. Lazarus was apparently in as good health as ever. He said his trance had hurt him no more than a long heavy sleep would have done. Of course there were many persons who worried him with questions as to whether during his trance he had seen anything of the unknown world or had fathomed any of the mysteries of the hereafter.

To such he would say: "You have heard that I had some sense of falling and that I believed I had landed in a cleft in an iceberg," then he would refer inquirers to Colonel Bob for a full explanation of the mental phenomena of his trance.

One day after Mr. Lazarus had made his reappearance on the street, I jokingly asked him whether from what he had seen of the realms of old Pluto he would be content to be permanently settled in them. To my surprise he looked very serious and said: "I was in a curious state and during that trance, brief as it was, saw that which would make volumes were all written out. What I saw and heard seems as real as anything that has ever happened to me at any time in my life, and I now remember all as distinctly as I do things that I have seen or heard to-day in this city. Though I have sent all who came to ask about my trance to Colonel Bob for an explanation, I do not mind telling you that I am firmly of the opinion that I in some way went forth in spirit, while my body was lying apparently lifeless, and obtained more than a mere glimpse of the things of the world beyond the grave. I have often had very vivid dreams, but this was a something much more connected and lifelike than any dream, and the things I saw and heard do not fade away and elude my mental grasp as is apt to be the case as regards the things of mere dreams. What I experienced has so clung to and worried me that I am now writing it all down, in order to try if I cannot get it out of my head by getting it upon paper."

Before parting with Mr. Lazarus I asked him if he would mind letting me see his vision of the things of the other world when he had written it out.

"Not at all," cried he cheerily, "indeed I'll make you a present of the manuscript if you would like it—you shall have it for old acquaintance sake. Also, I would wish some friend to have it for the reason that it appears to me to foreshadow something that is to happen to me; at least in part. Of course I do not expect all to fall out just as in my vision, but you know it is said that 'coming events cast their shadows before.'"

So we parted. Some days passed, then on going down town I was shocked to hear that my friend Lazarus had again fallen lifeless while walking along the street near his cottage. Again his brother Pacific Coast Pioneers took charge of the body, believing that their friend was not dead but had fallen in another fit and would revive in about thirty-six hours as before. Colonel Bob was quite confident that this would be the case, and whenever he was at the cottage where the body lay, which was the greater part of his time, he made it a point to do a great deal of loud talking, in order that his old friend might know that he was near. This failing he began addressing himself directly to his dead friend, shouting: "Lysander, I am here ready to help you. Do you know my voice? Come, wake up, your old friend Colonel Bob is here!"

The doctors, not one or two but half a dozen, had told the old Pioneers that this time their friend was really dead and there would be no revival, but they still had faith that life would presently return until decomposition obliged them to admit that all was indeed over.

The death of Lysander moved me much. It placed a weight upon my heart that the deepest sighs would not lift. I had known him in Nevada many years as an honest and industrious man, and also had known him in California in the days of placer mining. The latch-string of his cabin door was always on the outside. He was "generous to a fault" as the saying is, but was always much more generous to another's fault than to his own.

In his humble home every broken prospector traveling that way found a safe harbor. When an accident happened to a brother miner Lysander was always among the first to offer assistance. Many a sick and maimed miner was sheltered for weeks in his cabin. Rude as was his little log hut it was brighter in the eyes of many a man than the most stately mansion in the country.

The mortal remains of my dead friend were followed to the grave by a decent cortege of honest and respectable citizens in carriages, and behind the train of vehicles went marching two and two many an old pensioner of the deceased. In their hearts these men sincerely mourned the loss of the friend who had come to their aid in their many times of need.

A day or two after the funeral the Public Administrator informed me that he had found in the desk of Mr. Lazarus a large package addressed to me, which I could obtain by calling at his office. I was not surprised, on receiving the package, to find inscribed on the outside in the well-known hand of my dead friend the two words—"My Vision."

"His wision,"[3] said the Public Administrator, "I reckon that air dockerment contains an account of what he seed the fust time he died—I mean the time he laid in a tranct. I allers suspicioned that durin' that time he seed more'n he cared to tell of."

"It is probably something of the kind," said I.

"I thought so as soon as I seed it marked a wision. I've allers heerd that in a tranct a man gits a peep into t'other world; so, bein' curous that way, I'd like to have a squint at the dockerment when you git done with it, and I'll speak now for the fust loan of it."

Telling the man that in the course of time he would probably learn all about the document that it was necessary for him to know I left his office.

I give to the public the manuscript just as it came into my hands, without adding or subtracting a single word in any part. I know of no living person it can harm, and it appears to me to be too curious to be lost. A strange coincidence is that on the very day that Mr. Lazarus first fell as one dead news came from New York of the death in that city of the great financier and many times millionaire Magnificus Auriferous Dives, whose shade, as will presently appear, was companion to that of Lazarus in all its wanderings in the "world below." This circumstance almost constrains one to believe that what is related by Mr. Lazarus is a sketch of things and occurrences foreshadowing those which were soon to be real—as real as anything can be in a world of shades. Mr. Lazarus in his narrative at first speaks of his experience as if it were a vision or a dream, but presently he appears to feel as he advances in the recital of his adventures that he really was a shade wandering in the world of shades. He begins abruptly as follows:

Notes

1. This historical detail is correct and is therefore important in dating the text.
2. la grippe: another name for influenza.
3. This is an example of De Quille's attraction to Old Weller, a character from Dickens's *Pickwick Papers* who used such pronunciations as "wolatile" and "wiwacious." (See "Introduction," p. 30.)

Chapter I.
Terrors of the Grave—A Flight Through Space—Lazarus lands on "The Sunless Shore."

I dreamed or seemed to dream that I was dead; that I had been laid in my grave,[1] and had then risen in the spirit form and had crossed the "black infernal Styx" in the boat of old Charon, "grim ferryman of hell." I had a glimpse of the dark unknown that lies beyond the grave of that "undiscovered country, from whose bourn no traveler returns."[2]

As my body was being borne to the grave I felt great fear that there all would end; that my living spirit would there be forever imprisoned with my dead body. I felt an awful horror of that body—a mere disgusting thing of flesh that would fester and of bones that would slowly decay, while I, the real and living thing, would be imprisoned with that with which I had done—that which was no longer of me. Then as the hearse slowly rolled along, I thought of the lines of the poet, and over and over were pealed forth in tones deep and solemn as those of some mighty organ that filled all aerial space, the words—

> "Down through the yawning gulf, the grave,
> When life's brief fit is over,
>   Shall sink the great, the good, the brave,
> Down to the sunless shore,
>   Where, by the hush of sullen wave,
> They sleep for evermore."

It seemed to me that in this the old Greek poet meant to say that I must pass through the grave and thence to some dark region where I would forever remain amid myriads of shades in condition more dead than alive. That seemed very dreary and fearful, but not horrible, as would be remaining pent in the tomb with my cast-off mortal frame. The thought of lying forever in a state of semi-consciousness in some sunless place was very distressing, but I found that after my body had been deposited in the bosom of mother earth to return to that dust of which it was formed, another self arose from my old earthy shell. How long a time elapsed before this occurred I could not tell; but suddenly, to my surprise,

I found myself rising and floating in free aerial space. Night poured darkness down upon the earth. I feared I had entered that dark Cimmerian[3] desert, ''beyond the ocean stream,'' told of by the ancients—that place where the sun has never shone. ''Can it be,'' thought I, ''that I am going 'down to the sunless shore, to sleep for evermore by the hush of sullen wave'''?

Like a withered leaf, I was whirled through the air—whirled I knew not whither. I was much troubled for a time, but being utterly helpless I at last thought resignation to my fate the part of wisdom. In this frame of mind I said to myself: ''Though I seem to be aimlessly tossed about, now going upward and again downward, what matters it? There is in the universe neither up nor down. That is a mere notion of my own little planet; I must leave it behind with my old earthly tenement.'' I then commende my spirit to the keeping of the God of the Universe.

At last the utter darkness began to give way and, swiftly whirling through space, I came to a region of twilight, domed over by a ''doubtful sky.'' Through the dim light I saw that I was descending, and was drawing near to what had the appearance of an arm of a sea or a dark and sluggish river. Low and ragged hills of black lava bordered the single visible shore.

Notes

1. Inasmuch as Lazarus had not been buried, this appears to be an inconsistency in the text.

2. See *Hamlet* III, i, 79–80.

3. Cimmeria was a mythical land used by the Greeks as a commonplace for a region of darkness, remoteness, and bleakness.

Chapter II.
The River Styx—The Hoary old Boatman—The Rejected Passenger—A Voyage in Darkness amid Sighs and Whisperings—The Clutch of a Bony Hand—Ashore in a Beautiful Land.

"My God!" cried I, as I gazed about the dreary and unwholesome place—"My God, the river Styx!" Soon a sound of oars issued out of a bank of dark mist that hung along the water and reached almost to the slimy shore. Then pushed out from the dismal cloud a boatman old and hoary. "'Tis Charon!" I cried—"'Tis the Rower, old and dread, Ferryman of all the dead!"

Swiftly the boatman—gaunt, grim and gray—came on. Soon the prow of the boat touched the bending and unstable strand. Courageously I gazed full into the awful mummified face and said: "Son of Erebus,[1] I am come."

Without a word the old man held out to me his bony hand for his toll. For a moment I stood confused before the ancient ferryman, then I opened wide my mouth to show him that it contained no *obolus*—that I was an impecunious shade.[2] "Barbarian!" shouted the grim old man, as he bent forward and gazed down into the empty cavern that I presented for his inspection—"Barbarian to the gods unknown!" he cried in a tone of ineffable disdain.

At that moment, as I stood abashed before the ferryman of souls, there darted out from behind a little promontory of basaltic rock that jutted upon the beach near by, a being of an aspect strange and weird. It was a man remarkably tall and gaunt that I beheld, and he advanced toward the boat with long, swift, gliding strides. His hair hung in tangled and tossing locks far down his shoulders, and the beard that spread abroad upon his naked breast was even more huge than that of old Charon himself, but not so white—was merely dashed with gray. The face was that of a man of middle age, and the features were of a Bedouin cast; the complexion was of a bronze tint, verging upon the swart of the Ethiopian, and the small black eyes that peered out from great cavernous sockets had a strangely sad and eager expression.

I keenly scrutinized the features of this intruder, for his sudden appearance and stealthy gliding forward had a good deal startled me. Between ourselves, I feared that the weird personage might be Satan himself, come to make in my person an untimely snatch, and my relief was great when I saw no appearance of horns, hoofs or tail. Though wild looking, cadaverous and unkempt, the man before me had nothing in the expression of either face or eyes even in the smallest degree malicious; on the contrary there was stamped upon his countenance a look of the most utter hopelessness and weariness.

The Stygian ferryman did not appear to notice the presence of the uncanny stranger. In apparent disgust at finding my mouth empty of coin he had turned his face away and seemed absorbed in gazing out into the rolling mists of the river.

As the stranger came up to me he halted, and dropping his long staff into the hollow of his left arm began fumbling with his claw-like fingers at a pouch that hung from the girdle that confined at the loins his flowing mantle of brown woolen stuff. Soon he drew forth two coins, an *obolus* and a *danace*, and trembling with eagerness thrust them into my hand, whispering in a husky voice, with one eye upon the old boatman the while: "For me and thee—pay thou for both."

Thus saying the gaunt, desiccated old creature, who had proved the friend in need, flung aside his staff and darted into the boat with the agility of an ape. Crouching into the smallest possible space in the bow of the craft he drew over his face and head a fold of his mantle, when by some bit of physical and anatomical legerdemain withdrew within himself until he was visible only as an insignificant brown bundle.

While this was occurring the boatman of souls was still gazing abstractedly forth into the dark mists that were curling above the black waters of the infernal river. Touching him on the arm I handed him his toll. Motioning me aboard his craft, the old man seated himself and took up his oars.

Before he had made the first stroke, however—even before he had dipped his oars into the water—the old fellow seemed to recollect himself. He looked at the coins in his hand for a moment in a puzzled way, gazed hard at me—so hard that I felt as though about to resolve into a shade of even thinner material than that of which I was com-posed—then turned in his seat and gazed fixedly at the brown bundle wedged into the bow of the boat.

At sight of that bundle of tattered brown, the wrath of the hoary old ferryman was kindled. His eyes darted baleful fires from their cavernous depths, his nostrils quivered, and every muscle of his face so worked and writhed that even the beard on his shaggy jaws was agitated.

Springing to his feet the old boatman wrathfully threw upon the shore the two coins I had placed in his hands, and turning about like a flash he again fixed his fiery eyes upon that object in the bow of the boat which in outward appearance seemed a mere lifeless bundle; for no limb or feature of man, or ghost of man, was to be seen. Drawing himself to his full height, and still quivering with rage, old Charon cried in a shrill and fierce voice: "Ahasuerus, Kartaphilos, Salathiel ben Sadi, man by whatever other name known to men in the upper world, art thou here again? Crabbed cobbler of Jerusalem, must I again and for the thousandth time pitch thee from my boat?"

Not a sound came from the brown bundle, but I could see that it was agitated from beneath by a sort of shivering motion.

"Get off my boat, thou! Away with you—away, away!" screamed the irate old ferryman in a shrill and cracked voice. "Up and away! Did not the Man of Sorrows pronounce upon thee, O insolent cobbler, this sentence—'Tarry thou till I come?' Dost thou think to escape the expiation?"

So saying Charon pounced upon the cowering creature, and lifting him as though he had been a mere man of feathers, pitched him far out upon the shore, where he lay sprawling upon his face.

"Get thee hence," cried the ancient rower, bending his fierce relentless gaze upon the prostrate and motionless being—"Go wander through the regions of Earth; fulfill thy destiny as I do mine!" and he turned again to his oars.

Uttering but a single moan, the rejected passenger slowly arose. For a moment he stood gazing about in a bewildered way, then took up his long staff and strode out into the black mists that hovered along the oozy shore.

"That which I heard in the upper world," thought I, as I saw the tall weird figure disappear amid rolling wreaths of fog, "was not mere fable; there is going about upon the face of the earth such a wretched being as he who is known to men as the 'Wandering Jew.'"[3]

Having rid himself of the forbidden passenger, Charon's face soon resumed its accustomed calm. I had feared that the next move of the irate old man would be to pitch me neck and heels out of his boat to wander for untold ages along the dismal shore, but he did not deign to so much as bestow a single glance upon me, ignorant barbarian as I was in his eyes.

Seating himself in his boat the aged ferryman laid himself to his oars and the crank[4] and creaking craft sped over the surface of the steaming waters like an arrow. Backward streamed the white hair of the old man as we dashed through the dank and ill-smelling mists. His eyes were closed as though he had fallen asleep. As I gazed at him from my place in the stern of the boat, he seemed more as one of the old Egyptian kings, dead and entombed in the pyramids three thousand years, than a living thing; yet his oars whirled so steadily and so swiftly that they resembled the spokes of a rapidly revolving wheel, and the boat seemed to hold its course by some inherent virtue, just as the needle points to the Pole.

Soon we entered mists so thick and black that the darkness was total. Not a breath of air was moving. I could no longer hear the strokes of the old ferryman's oars, but my ears were filled with sounds a thousand times more disagreeable. All about me I could hear sighs and whisperings, once a long wail was uttered in my very face, and once I felt a bony hand clutching at me.

Presently the blackness gave way to a thick warm mist that was filled with a bright phosphorescent light, yet was impenetrable to my sight. Neither shore was visible and no landmark was to be seen. I could not so much as see the old boatman, or the boat in which I was seated, but I saw hundreds of faces—awful, livid faces. They were above and all about me, and many came so near that their faces almost touched mine.

Whether these creatures were Harpies, Furies,[5] or mere shades of mortals I knew not, but at times when one of the corpse-like faces was thrust into mine I felt a chill in the place where my spine would have been had I not been a mere unsubstantial ghost.

Again we entered a dark zone and the myriads of faces disappeared, but only to be replaced by a bewildering din of cries, groans and such shrieks of agony that all the murders ever done from the beginning of the world seemed being re-enacted. At times jets of flame burst upward from the bosom of the stream, giving a brief glimpse of the black water and of tossing arms and agony-distorted faces.[6]

How long we were in these awful regions I know not. It might have been moments, or it might have been days, months or years. I could not judge of time, for there were periods when I lost all consciousness—seemed to be completely annihilated. Again for long periods of time I was in a dream-like state, when the awful din about me took on the form of a mere uniform roar, as of a great storm or the bellowing and booming of the sea.

At last I beheld breaking upward through the blackness of the Stygian mists long, brilliant lances of light, such as at times illuminate the Boreal regions of our planet Earth. An instant after and there was a burst of such light as has never shone "on sea or land" in our upper world. Then rose into view, as though out of a world of waters and golden haze, a bright and beautiful land.

The boat grazed the strand as I gazed, and as the wonders of that land began to unfold in a thousand varying forms I leaped ashore and with hands lifted above my head, like a delighted child, I cried: "Great God, I thank thee!" As my hungry eyes roved abroad for refreshment in the green and fruitful region before me I found myself, without thought of what I was doing, quoting from Wilhelm Meister—

> "Know'st thou the land where lemon-trees do bloom,
> And oranges like gold in leafy gloom;

The myrtle thick, and high the laurel grows?
Know'st thou it, then?"[7]

I then bethought myself and turned to thank the ancient boatman, but he had disappeared. Silently and swiftly he had turned his craft and pulled away. Back into the dark and rolling mists of the infernal river had sped that

"Rower old and dread,
Ferryman of the dead."

Notes

1. Erebus was the god of darkness. By extension, the word also refers to the underworld.

2. All dead souls, according to Greek mythology, had to be ferried across the river Styx on their way to Hades, which was not Hell but only the realm of the dead. Each soul had to pay a small coin—usually an *obolus*—to the ferryman Charon.

3. According to the legend of the Wandering Jew, a Jew of Jerusalem struck Jesus on the way to Calvary and shouted in mockery: "Go faster, Jesus, go faster. Why do you loiter?" Jesus looked at him and said, "I am going, but you shall wait until I return." The Jew, whom tradition has given several names, was thenceforth unable to die, though he sought death, and has since wandered restlessly over the earth.

4. crank: a nautical term meaning "unstable," "likely to capsize."

5. Both Harpies and Furies were mythological hostile female monsters. The Furies were associated with vengeance.

6. These details do not appear in most mythological sources; De Quille may have adapted them from Dante's *Inferno*.

7. Mignon's song, from Goethe's *Wilhelm Meister*, as translated by Thomas Carlyle.

Chapter III.
A Region of Wonderful Beauty—The Shade of Dives Appears—Dives Talks of His Good Works—Beckoning Shades—The Wrong Road.

Turning again toward the beautiful land, I felt myself impelled to advance into it. Step by step I was enticed forward by the new beauties that each moment unfolded themselves. All the attractions of grove, of stream, and of flowery mead with songs of birds enticed me forward. These varied delights of the eye and all the other senses seemed to increase along a broad and easy path that led toward where there shone in the upper air, apparently at a vast distance, a light more roseate and bright than was to be seen in any other quarter, and, almost without thought, I wandered thitherward. Often as I strolled along I was tempted to stretch myself upon the velvet grass beneath some tree of wondrous foliage. Among the boughs of these strangely beautiful trees sang birds from whose throats were poured such liquid and tuneful notes as I had never heard approached by even the sweetest instruments of human invention in the old weary mechanical upper world. In listening to the joyous and soul-soothing music of the songsters of the groves I halted and lingered at every turn of the path. New beauties were constantly coming into view and why should I not drink them all in and fill my heart with them? There was no reason for even a thought of haste; I was done with time—before me lay eternity.

Presently, while I was reclining upon a gentle swell of ground beneath a palm-like tree that grew beside the path, delightedly listening to the music of a large golden-winged and emerald-crested bird that had a voice like a flute, I beheld approaching from the way of the ferry of the dead a form which I at once recognized as that of a man of Earth, and a product of these latter days. Said I, as I propped myself on my elbows and closely scrutinized the approaching shade: "A man from the domain of Uncle Sam hitherward comes, or he lies in his astral shape. He is given away by his Harrison hat."[1]

As the shade drew near I recognized it as being that of Magnificus Auriferous Dives, a man of millions whom I had known, though rather at a distance, in the upper world. Dives was a man of whom it might be said that through him all life's generous impulses had leaked as through a sieve; gold and vast possessions alone had power to cause a throb in his sordid heart.

Gaily he advanced, and I noticed that already he had plucked and placed in his button-hole a "fair undying narcissus flower," all "bathed in heaven's ambrosial dew." With head erect he was glancing to right and left as he rushed along, evidently well pleased with the fair scene and probably mentally figuring upon its value per acre as a place of winter resort.

As Hon. M. Auriferous Dives thus sped along, casting far abroad his speculative gaze, he was on the point of passing without seeing me. I arose and greeting him with a friendly "hello," asked him whither he was bound.

"Why, hello! Glad to see you here," said Dives—"Well, as you may see, I'm on my way to Heaven. It is quite a surprise, however, to see you here; yet I believe that all kinds of people—black, yellow and red as well as white—are ferried over and landed here en route to Heaven."

"Is not this Heaven?" I asked.

"This Heaven! Pooh! No; and I am surprised that you should think so. Why, my dear fellow, this is merely the garden of the Hesperides, the Elysian Fields,[2] or other such out-lying and suburban place."

"Whatever it may be," said I, "it is a glad and beautiful place, and I would that the Master would permit me to remain in it."

"Yes, this is pretty fair; and of course it's quite valuable, being so near to the Celestial City, which must grow rapidly now that the true religion is spreading and is even being carried into Africa, China and other populous regions. It may soon become necessary to set apart an African quarter somewhere out this way, or to make room out in this suburb for a Chinatown."

"I feel," said I, "that this is a better and a more enchanting place than I have deserved and I am astonished that in his goodness God has permitted me to see it."

"Of course, this is all very fine," said Dives, "but every one may not feel inclined to take up with it when it is known that there is better ahead; more especially when one feels that one has done that which merits the earliest recognition and the highest reward. This place may do for some—for such as have never had any very high aspirations—and, now that I think of it, this may be the Limbo of Dante; a place for blameless pagans of ancient times, and for unbaptized babes and sucklings. It may even be the Limbus Fatuorum—the Limbo of Fools, or Fool's Paradise. I have read that there is such a place."

"It seems a good and a beautiful land," said I, glancing abroad over the flowery meads, meandering brooks and musical groves, "and I, for one, would be fool enough to rejoice to dwell in it forever, if the good God would let me."

"Bah! What are you talking about?" cried Dives—"You are just the same here as when in the flesh; ready to put up with whatever comes to you. Come along with me to the Celestial City—I'll rig a purchase to get you in. As a member of Congress I've had a good deal of useful experience at Washington, you know. Of course things here will be a little different—must here be given a somewhat different turn, you see. But, happen what may, I fancy that you'll be permitted to go in with me as my servant, if I request it as a favor—and you know that you did once work for me a short time. No doubt the matter can be fixed in that way."

As we moved onward across a vast grove-dotted plain that lay before us Magnificus became quite talkative. He seemed in excellent spirits. He told me that he felt confident that he had finally done a very wise thing, though at the time—even while doing it—he was a little afraid he was acting foolishly. This referred to the disposition he had made of his wealth. He said that when all the doctors had consulted and told him he was on his death bed, he began to seriously feel that the time had come when he must in some way dispose of his accumulated millions, since he could not carry the gold with him.

He said he at first ran over in his mind his many poor relations, but it seemed to him that they were all "rather a shiftless set"; then he thought of the many poor men and women that had at various times been in his employ, but as he had always paid them all he had agreed to pay, he did not think they had any claim upon him; and should he give them anything they would no doubt become idle and worthless. Clearly to give to such people would do no good and might do harm.

In short, after thoroughly revolving the matter in his mind, Magnificus arrived at the conclusion, as he informed me, that having acquired his wealth through his own exertions and sagacity—and not being able to take it with him to the grave—the best he could do would be to so dispose of it that it would count for the benefit of his soul whither he was going. With a sagacious wink, looking about him and lowering his voice, he then said: "Thus, you see, my dear fellow, I was really, in a way, carrying my gold into this new world; or rather sending it ahead to be placed to my credit in the Celestial City."

"How did you manage this matter so neatly?" I asked.

"O, it's no new thing—no new invention," said Magnificus—"After cudgeling my brains in vain for a long time, I fell back upon the old, time-honored dodge."

"I do not understand you," said I.

"No?" said Magnificus and with much gusto he then set to work and gave me the full list of the amounts he had left by will to a great variety of institutions. There was $500,000 each to this church and that—no denomination being wholly neglected—$300,000 each to missions in Africa and China, $1,000,000 for a library in New York, $500,000 for a school in

Boston, and amounts ranging from $100,000 to $250,000 for hospitals and I know not what other institutions; but the list concluded, if memory serves me aright, with a bequest of $150,000 for founding a hospital for cats without claws. As there would be the Dives Library, the Dives University, and the Dives this and Dives that, Magnificus requested me to note that he had taken care that several monuments should be erected to his memory in prominent places.

We had journeyed a great distance and had seen but little of the beauties of the region through which we were passing, so long was the list of benefactions which Dives had to recite. When he had ceased to regale my ears with his history of good deeds done in the flesh, and we again lifted our eyes to note the landscape we found many things to interest us. The scenery had greatly changed, and was, if possible, even more beautiful than any we had yet seen. Also we now for the first time saw the shades of men and women in places where there were little temples, bowers and fountains among the groves.

In one place several shades standing in the portico of a large temple, that appeared to be of white marble, beckoned us to come to them. I called the attention of Dives to the shades, all of those standing forth appearing to be noble and angelic beings, and suggested that they probably had information of importance to impart to us, but he cried: "No; let them beckon. We do not want to make the acquaintance of such as live out here in the suburbs—they are no doubt rather a low set, or are a lot of idiots."

As we walked on admiring the beauties of the changeful landscape and listening to the music of the birds, we for the first time bethought ourselves that we had seen no sun in this heavenly land. The light came alike from all parts of a luminous dome that occupied the place of the sky of our old planet Earth. This light, though bright, was soft and beautiful. Brighter far, and more roseate, than this general light from the dome was the far-away light I have before mentioned; but this last light Dives either could not or would not see, though I repeatedly pointed it out and told him we were leaving it too far to the left. This I did not like, as I believed it a light placed for the guidance of the shades of mortals landing on the shores of this unknown world.

Notes

1. Opponents of President Benjamin Harrison (Rep. 1889–92) sometimes caricatured him as wearing the antique and overly large hat of his grandfather, President William Henry Harrison. The implication was that the grandson was not the man his grandfather was. Although Harrison seemed favorable to silver, he did not pursue the free silver issue vigorously enough for silverites like De Quille. When Harrison lost the 1892 presidential campaign to Cleveland, an opponent of free silver, De Quille wrote that silverites would not notice any practical difference in federal policy. The Harrison hat therefore probably hints at Dives's betrayal of silver and the masses.

2. The Elysian Fields were believed by the ancient Greeks to be the dwelling place of happy souls after death. They were variously located on the western edge of the earth, or in the underworld. The Hesperides, used here as an equivalent, were sometimes called the Fortunate Isles. They were a fabled group of lovely islands, also located in the uttermost West.

Chapter IV.
An Uncanny Region—No Return—Strange Creatures Materialize—Dives in Trouble—The "Kitchen-Middens" of Hell.

Our path presently began to lead down a declivity which by almost imperceptible degrees grew in steepness. As we proceeded the path became winding, and at every turn steeper, though it everywhere remained smooth and broad.

Magnificus suddenly halted and turning to me said: "Strange that I did not think of it before, but is it not simply beastly that carriages are not provided to carry persons from the ferry to the city? Then the ferry itself is an abomination—nothing but a crazy old canoe, with a miserable half-witted old man to paddle it. There ought to be a good steam ferry-boat there, a competent pilot and electric lights, for the place is miserably dark and foggy; not to speak of it being full of yowling idiots, devils, hell-hags or something of the kind."

"If you come to that," said I, "why not go in at once for a railroad from the ferry on the Styx to the Celestial City?"[1]

"By Jove, I was just thinking of that, and as soon as I get to the city and get settled, I shall propose it to the authorities. In the meantime, however, vehicles of some kind might be put upon this road. I suppose that they still have a few of those old chariots somewhere about the city? I'm pretty sure that I've heard or read about one of 'em being sent out for the accommodation of Elijah."[2]

While Dives thus pleasantly discoursed I observed that the landscape had gradually grown more austere. First the flowers had disappeared, then the foliage-laden trees with their colonies of singing birds, and at last the emerald of the lawns and parks was replaced with brown and stunted herbage. Huge black rocks made their appearance at the turns in the path as it wound down the declivity and the air began to grow dusky. I called the attention of Magnificus to these changes.

He looked about in a frightened way and then cried: "Well, we've lost our way! While you were chattering about railroads and chariots, we somewhere took a wrong turn. When one is obliged to trudge about on foot in a strange place there ought at least to be a guide furnished one!"

"It was, perhaps, because we were observed to be going astray that the people we saw off to the left hand by the white temple beckoned us," said I.

"Perhaps it was," said Dives sullenly, "but why didn't the idiots come down to us and put us on the right road?"

"Let us turn back," said I, "and ask them to point out to us the direct road to the Celestial City. We must have missed it at some turn in that place of many groves and thick shrubbery."

We faced about with the intention of retracing our steps, but to our surprise and consternation the path behind us was found to be blocked by a perpendicular cliff of basalt—a cliff so high that its top was lost in the dusk that brooded over and filled the place.

The cliff stood squarely across the path down which we had just passed and as Dives gazed upon it his jaw fell. He placed his hand upon it and drawing back cried: "It has just arisen. It is hot—quite hot! It cannot be that we are going headlong into that beastly place they call Hell?"

"It looks and smells very much like it," said I, for just then there was wafted on the breeze an odor that certainly was not from the "spicy shore of Arabie the blest."

"Virgil was right," said I:—

———"Facilis descensus Averni: Sed revocare gradum superasque evadere ad aures, Hoc opus, hic labor est."[3]

Magnificus stood staring at the rock as I thus recited, and finally said: "It don't move a particle. Your hog-Latin open sesame, or whatever sort of charm you was muttering didn't move it a single inch."

"It was no charm," said I, "but an awful truth which I now realize as never before. It runs thus as translated by an English poet:

> "Avernus' gates are open night and day,
> Smooth the descent, and easy is the way:
> But to return to heaven's pure light again,
> This is a work of labor and of pain."

"Well, let us see what can be done," said Dives.

"I don't mind the labor and pain if we can but get out of this beastly hole."

My reply was: "Miseriarum portus est patienti," that is "Patience is the asylum of the afflicted."[4]

"Come," cried Dives—"come, why will you stand there mumbling and rolling up your eyes at that confounded rock? Ugh! I have no patience with a man who can stand quoting poetry in hell!"

"And I have my opinion," I retorted, "of a man who comes strutting into hell wearing a Harrison hat!"

"That is better than your—but, hist! I heard a laugh somewhere," said Dives lowering his voice—"there are devils about. Let us not fall into a quarrel in this awful place. You got me into it, now get me out of it."

"I got you into it! If either was at fault it was yourself. The shades that signaled us to turn toward them, on the left, no doubt wished to show us that thitherward lay our way. We have probably taken a wrong turn and got into the pagan hell. Now that I think of it an old Greek has a poem entitled 'The Right-hand Road to Hades.' In mourning the death of a friend the old poet says—

'That right-hand path thy pensive ghost pursued,
Loved Aristonous! when it left behind
Those not unmindful of the great and good,
Eternal joys among the blest to find.'"[5]

"I'm blest," cried Dives, "if this either looks or smells like the way to the realms of the blest and eternal joys. I'm confoundedly afraid, my dear fellow, that we've got into that beastly old—but, mum! I hear whispers in the rock. Let us go a little smooth—policy my boy! (This was whispered in my ear, then elevating his voice.) For my own part I never believed the—that is his Satanic Majesty, so bad as he has been represented by certain long-faced if not two-faced gentlemen. There are always two sides to a story. No doubt but His Majesty of these realms had grievances, and great one. (Here Dives nudged me with his elbow.) And no doubt suffered wrongs at the hands of—I would say wrongs that we know not of," and Dives rolled his eyes about as though half expecting to see the face of the devil grinning at him from over the top of one of the blocks of lava that bordered the path.

"In your will, Mr. Dives," said I, "you ought to have left a few hundred thousand to erect a chapel to the devil."

"Peace! Let us give no cause of offense in this place," whispered Dives huskily.

Seeing that Dives was really in a great fright I changed the subject by saying: "As we cannot return, there is nothing for it but to advance."

Turning again to the path that led onward we found it still broad and smooth, but while we had tarried to lament our sad situation the rocks on each side of it had imperceptibly risen and now formed towering perpendicular walls. Before us there seemed to lie a vast valley region, but it was so shrouded in misty gloom that no object was visible by which we could judge of its nature. Downward and directly into this undiscoverable valley led our path, and silently and with sinking hearts we took our way into it; Dives gently placing me in the lead.

As we advanced the gloom increased and soon it became dismal. It was not blackness, but that awful, ghostly kind of light seen on Earth during a total eclipse of the sun. All objects before and about us, for the short distance we could see, were tinged with a hue such as is seen on looking through a sheet of brown glass.

The region was more abominable than the deserts of Hesebon and Philarioth. The only vegetation visible was in the shape of gigantic fungi that at a distance, in the haze of the place, resembled Chinamen in their huge umbrella hats. These on a near view were seen to be dripping a foul black dew. Other species were so tall and of a form so peculiar that they reminded me of the melancholy groups of tree cactus seen in those great deserts to which the Mexicans give the name of *jornadas del muerto*.[6] Many of the toadstool variety of fungi, all dripping with deadly dews, rose before our eyes at the edge of the path and by crowding into line showed that to some extent they possessed the power of locomotion; I even saw one that was knocked over get up and resume its place. As it did so I was quite sure that I saw it show for an instant a wrinkled and comical-looking face.

I began to feel quite certain that in this dank and dismal region we had wandered into one of hell's waste places—a sort of suburb in which dwelt monsters of divers breeds. Dives complained bitterly of the dampness and declared he would "take his death of cold." But soon new and greater terrors seized his soul.

Huge slimy serpents began to be seen crossing our path, halting a moment to lift their heads and gaze at us with fiery eyes. In one place a creature like a land crab, which had a great hole beside the path reached out with a pair of claws so huge that they extended across the whole width of the path and making a snap at me came near gathering in poor Dives, who was close behind. The creature was large enough to have carried off an ox. Also winged reptiles of the dragon species now and again flew through the air with tremendous spread of wing and amazing noise.

At last after an unusually large and particularly noisy flock of these creatures had passed over our heads with a roar resembling that of Niagara, Dives suddenly seated himself and took his face between his hands.

He had dropped down upon a boulder of black lava that lay beside the path and appeared to be completely broken down. He complained to having been duped "by persons who called themselves men of God."

"I can now see," said Dives bitterly, "how finely I have been trapped. I was told that all my bequests would count for the good of my soul, but now, after loading them all with my gold, here I am in hell among snakes, flying alligators and infernal creatures. I have been woefully—"

Dives did not finish his sentence for all at once the black boulder on which he was seated took on the shape of a monster mole and began to walk off with him on its back. The thing had almost reached its den—a great black hole beside the path—before Dives discovered that he was being carried off.

I pulled Dives back upon the trail the moment he called for help and we again moved on. He slouched along behind me utterly without hope; declaring it was useless to proceed, yet afraid to halt. In addition to the strong-winged dragons that circled about aloft we presently began to see winging their way about us creatures with the faces of old women. They had bat-like wings and in their flight were as noiseless as owls. They were evidently of the Harpy family, but they did us no further harm than to float softly in out of the dusk and peer keenly into our faces. They certainly did not speak well for the holiness of the place.

The appearance and the actions of these creatures caused Dives to again break down. "This settles it!" said he. "Decidedly we are in hell or these old hens would not be hovering about. We may as well stop right here—to go farther will be to fare worse."

I reminded him of his late experience in stopping at the boulder, and told him of the light I had seen at such a height and distance that it must rise in a place far beyond and above the deep and dismal valley we were then in. Dives feared that the light was but the reflection of the fires of some latter part of Satan's domain, but consented to move on—particularly as he found the ground breaking away behind him and flames coming up.

We now moved at a rapid pace, for there were many quakings of the ground and spoutings of jets of fire.

Notes

1. Nathaniel Hawthorne's "The Celestial Railroad" (1843) is an ironic story on this topic.
2. See *I Kings* 2:9–12.
3. *The Aeneid*, Book VI.
4. To be correct, the quotation should read "miserorum."
5. This is from a poem attributed to Hegesippus in *The Greek Anthology*, 7.545. For a prose translation, see the Loeb Classical Library.
6. Lit. "journeys of death."

Chapter V.
The Hall of Minos—A Grand White-Haired Old Man—Mercury—Nyx and Other Immortals—Pleasant Wanderings in Hades.

Presently as we sped along in the gloom of the dismal plain we heard a deep baying of dogs. This was to us a welcome sound—almost as cheering as though we had heard the voices of human beings. Advancing in the direction whence the sounds proceeded, we soon came to a magnificent hall of black marble. Though the atmosphere was still somewhat lurid, we were glad to find that we were leaving behind what might be termed the kitchen-middens of hell and entering upon a part of the plain that had a more stable and less forbidding appearance, yet we approached the great hall with timidity and hesitation.

Before the portico of the hall lay a three-headed dog larger than a bull sea lion. Many snakes, alert and out-reaching, writhed about the triple neck of the canine monster, and over his back was curled a sting-armed tail like that of a scorpion.

Within the open portico upon a great raised seat of ivory and ebony sat a grand white-haired old man.

"It is the tribunal of Minos," said I, as we halted and gazed in awe. "It is as I had begun to suspect; we have wandered into Hades—into the infernal region of the ancient Greeks and Romans."

"Any hell for me," said Dives, "but the regular orthodox one—the Christian hell. That is the one I wish to steer clear of. But, who is the old man mounted upon the throne above that damnable dog?"

"That is Minos," said I, "son of Jupiter and Europa, and one of the three judges in this lower world.[1] I believe it will be necessary for us to go before him and make confession."

"Make confession!" cried Dives, aghast—"What kind of confession?"

"Why, a full confession of all our actions while on Earth. This great judge then pronounces the sentence of either happiness or misery demanded by our good or evil deeds. If our actions through life have been good we take the right hand way to the Elysian Fields; if bad we go to Tartarus, a place as far below this as heaven is above the earth in our old world.[2] The judge looks like a very benevolent personage, and when on Earth, as king of Crete, had a world-wide reputation for wisdom and justice."

"I want none of him!" cried Dives, with death in his face—"He'll be too severe. Let me go back among the flying alligators and bat-winged old hags!" and Dives turned to retreat but to his great consternation found his feet glued to the ground.

While Dives was still explaining to me this new source of terror the god Mercury, with a great whizzing of the wings at his heels, alighted from the upper air and stood directly before us. Touching his winged silver cap with his wand, the messenger god politely informed us that it would not be required of us to go before either of the awful judges of Hades; that being natives of a Christian land we would be passed upon in another place.

We then walked past the dog Cerberus,[3] who at the appearance of Mercury had coiled down with his heads between his paws, and who took no further notice of us than to roll upon us three pairs of ugly red eyes. Even the snakes had subsided and the great jointed tail had sheathed its poniard-like sting. The grand face of Minos was as calm and unreadable as that of the sphinx, and the grave eyes appeared not to see us as we quickly glided by his gloomy judgement hall.

No sooner were we out of ear-shot than Dives, heaving a sigh of relief, said: "By Jove, I'm glad we're past old Judge Minos! Do you know I didn't at all like his looks? He had the look of one of your hanging kind of judges. No policy about him; he'd stick to the letter of the law. But who was the handsome young fellow that told us we could pass?"

"That was Hermes."

"Who?"

"Hermes, otherwise known as Mercury. He is the herald of the other gods, also the guide of all shades through this region in which we now are—even Hades. Though reputed tricky and a great thief he certainly did us a good turn."

"Good turn! I guess he did. By Jove, there's some style about that fellow! I wish he had remained with us. What did he steal?"

I entertained Dives with some of the thievish tricks of the god, and when I had concluded he said: "O, he's merely a mischievous sort of fellow. I at first thought he might be one who went in for something solid. Well, it is fortunate after all that he did not come with us. He'd probably have played us some trick that would have made us look ridiculous," and at once Dives lost all interest in the winged-god.

As we pursued our way the sallow light of the place gradually faded out and soon we found ourselves in darkness so utter that we were obliged to halt. In the midnight blackness a great rumbling sound was heard approaching and a moment later a tall and beautiful woman with a long veil streaming back from her queenly head dashed by in a chariot drawn by two black horses. A train of stars attended and followed her, lighting up her way.

"By Jove, a devilish fine woman!" cried Dives—"Was it Venus?"

"No. It was one of a far different mold and temper," said I. "It was Nyx—the goddess of Night."

"Night?"

"Yes; mother of the twin brothers, Thanatos and Hypnus—Death and Sleep."

"Mother of twins! Then she is a married woman?"

"Yes; she is reported to have been married to Erebus."

"Ah! only reported to have been married! It would seem that these goddesses are tricky—much the same as some of the lesser kind that we have known."

"There is no nonsense about this one. See, she is just driving into the courtyard of her palace. How grand it looks as its towering front is lighted up by the attendant stars!"

"It does, by Jove! Don't you know, my dear fellow, it looks like some of the old castles I visited at when I was in England. Wonder if we couldn't invent some excuse to call on the lady? But I don't believe I've a solitary card about me. How deuced unfortunate!"

"Console yourself, Mr. Dives," said I, "though we may not venture to call upon the mother, we may make bold to take a look at the residence of her two sons, which is hard by. Now that I know that we are actually in Hades I am not wholly at sea. The dwelling stands here to the left, partly encircled by an arm of Lethe, and enshrouded in perpetual twilight."

We found the mansion, half cavern half palace, built into the face of a cliff that rose upon the beach of a murmuring branch of the river whose waters bring forgetfulness to all who quaff thereof. About the portals of the palace were beds of tall poppies and other plants of kinds begetting somnolence, and the dew upon which, in evaporating as it distilled, filled with drowsiness the air of all the silent vale.

The palace stood open to the view—

> "No door there was, the unguarded house to keep,
> On creaking hinges turn'd, to break his sleep.
> But in the gloomy court was raised a bed,
> Stuff'd with black plumes, and on an ebon 'sted;
> Black was the covering too, where lay the god,
> And slept supine, his limbs display'd abroad;
> About his head fantastic visions fly,
> Which various images of things supply."

As we stood silently gazing in upon the immortal sleeper, Hypnus, his twin brother, Thanatos, suddenly appeared, or rather materialized, and hovered silently and lovingly about the couch of the slumberer. The god of Death held in his hand his inverted torch and so fair was he to behold, and so youthful, that Dives whispered: "By Jove, Cupid! He has come to whisper in the ears of the young fellow who is sleeping some dream of love, I fancy."

When I tell Dives that the beautiful youth is Death, he is slow to believe it. He has always imagined Death as a frightful being; a skeleton with fiery eyes blazing deep in the sockets of his skull and a dart poised in his hand. I tell him that Death is in appearance beautiful to those whose days on earth have been well spent. Why should he be otherwise than young and fair? He is the bright messenger sent to conduct the suffering and labor-worn to realms of bliss and to a new and eternal life. As old Aesop says:

> "Who, but for Death, could find repose
> From life, and life's
> unnumbered woes?
> From ills that mock our art to cure,
> As hard to fly as to endure."

Beautiful should be to us the countenances, and beautiful on the mountains the feet of those who bring to us good tidings;[4] therefore to the truly good man and real believer in the life to come, Death is merely the bright messenger who comes to lead him forth to his reward. The ancient Greek sculptors always represented Death as a beautiful youth. This was probably because the artists were men of education and men who had been initiated into the Eleusinian Mysteries,[5] in which we are told lessons of the highest moral character were taught, and the souls of those who participated in them were filled with "the sweetest hopes both as to this and the future world"; and it was a common saying among the Athenians: "In the Mysteries no one is sad."

All these things I said, and how long I should have thus gone on speaking in praise of the good angel, Death, I know not, had I not been cut short by Dives, who cried impatiently: "Say no more. I am quite disgusted with him, bright and fine as he looks. He is the meddlesome fellow who got me into a bad box—who made me fill my house with anxious religionists and hungry long-haired fellows who called themselves lovers of both dogs and men—the fellow who hustled me off here when I was just getting things into shape to enjoy life. Let us get out of this; I loathe the sight of the fellow!"

In leaving the grounds surrounding the house of Sleep, we saw pass near us his son Morpheus, god of dreams. He moved slowly and noiselessly along with closed eyes, bearing in his hand a cluster of poppies the seeds of which he scattered broadcast before him.

"There, now," cried Dives, "is a fellow that I could have heartily welcomed always, even had he come to me every night; but that uncle of his in coming but the one time was the death of me."

Wandering onward we presently came into a picturesque region of mountains, streams, groves and valleys where there was everywhere diffused a soft and pleasant light. Strolling up a dell we came to the "shadowing crag" on a mountainside at the base of which in a cavern dwells Chiron, "wisest and greatest of all the Centaurs." To adopt the language of the poet—

> "We enter'd straight a grot,
>   of gloomy twilight shade,
> There on a lowly couch
>   The Centaur huge was laid.
> At length unmeasured stretched
>   his rapid legs were thrown;
> And shod with horny hoofs
>   reclined upon the stone."

One look was all that Dives remained to take. As soon as we were at a safe distance he cried: "He's a beastly creature! but, by Jove, in the upper world he alone would make the fortune of a dozen Barnums.[6] There, my dear boy, only to think of the flying alligators, the old women—all head and bat wings—and the big crawfish that made a grab at my leg!"

"And the big ground mole that came near carrying you into its hole," said I.

Notes

1. According to Plato's *Apology*, 41a, there were at least four "true judges" of the world below: Minos, Rhadamanthus, Aeacus, and Triptolemus.

2. De Quille appears to be following the *Aeneid*, Book VI. The Sibyl there guides Aeneas to the right-hand fork of the crossroad, for it leads to Elysium, whereas the left descends to Tartarus. This direction is not a contradiction to the earlier allusion to "The Right-Hand Road to Hades," which occurs at an earlier stage of the trip and refers to a different junction.

3. Cerberus was a three-headed dog that guarded the entrance to Hades.

4. See *Isaiah* 52:7.

5. A salvation cult that worshipped Demeter, the goddess of agriculture, fertility, and marriage, at Eleusis.

6. P. T. Barnum (1810–91), famous American showman who specialized in exhibiting freaks, unusual animals, and other curiosities.

Chapter VI.
The Treasure-House of Plutus—Dives quite Overcome—He introduces Himself to the God of Riches—Plutus fires Dives out of His Cavern.

Next, at Dives' urgent request we bent our steps to the cavern of Plutus, god of riches. It was found at the foot of a second great mountain in the neighborhood, in a spot where three valleys met and

> "Where the river wanders o'er sands of gold,
> Where the burning rays of the ruby shine,
> And the diamond lights the secret mine,
> And the pearl gleams forth from the coral strand."

Over the door of the cavern—a door arched with huge ribs of solid gold—was the following inscription in letters of large size, all composed of precious stones of various hues:—

"Seek not Proud Riches, but Such as thou mayest get Justly, Use Soberly, Distribute Cheerfully, and leave Contentedly."

As we stood before the cavern Dives read this inscription aloud. He read it twice and with a very rueful countenance. Apparently he could scarcely credit the evidence of his eyes. Not a word was there that was not to him a direct slap in the face.

"By Jove," said he at last, "rather peculiar sentiments for one who is supposed to have heaped up in his vaults more wealth than is to be found in one spot elsewhere in all the universe. 'Distribute cheerfully and leave contentedly,'" muttered he, again casting his eyes upon the inscription. "That's rather tough on a fellow, don't you know. By Jove, according to those rules, what's the use of toiling and scheming to rake together fifteen or twenty millions?"

"What is the use," I asked, "of heaping up millions under your own rule?"

Dives winced, but pretending not to hear said: "Deuced queer, too, that with gold in all the streams, and rubies glittering all about in the mines, not a guard is to be seen anywhere, and even the door of this mighty treasure-house stands open!"

"And add to this," said I, "that the master of all this wealth is blind."

"Blind!" cried Dives.

"Blind, and besides is a mere child."[1]

"And a little blind boy has charge of all this wealth?" asked Dives.

"Sole charge. Doubtless his understanding flows from the eternal fountain of wisdom. You remember that at twelve years of age the child Christ disputed with the doctors in the temple at Jerusalem."[2]

Passing through the portal of that which outwardly appeared to be a cavern, we found within a grand hall of noble proportions. The high domed roof of the great cathedral-like structure was supported upon magnificent arches that rose on all sides from the main walls. These arches were of polished jasper, porphyry, malachite and lapis lazuli, thickly ribbed, bossed and twined with the precious metals. At the meeting point of the arches in the center of the dome was set as a keystone a single diamond of such great size as could be imagined only by one of the grand old califs of those days of magnificent things in which Haroun al Raschid[3] lived and reigned; and could only have been polished and lifted to its place by beings having the craft and power of the mighty genii who were invoked by Aladdin and other heroes of the "Arabian Nights."

This huge gem was as a sun to the great treasure-hall, and its dazzling light was reflected in all the colors of the solar spectrum by the rubies, emeralds, sapphires, carbuncles, amethysts and other precious stones set in the bosses and the vine and flower-work of the arches, panels and friezes.

Ingots and wedges of gold were heaped along the walls of one side of the treasure-house and with them chests of coins in the same metal from all the mints of the universe; both ancient and modern. There were even loose heaps of gold coin on the marble floor, as though the coffers had overflown. On the opposite side of the hall were piled massive bars of silver, with many huge chests of silver coins, while from the mouth of a great arched passage coin of silver had flown out and spread abroad upon the floor, as if from some vast vault in the heart of the mountain.

Diamonds in a thousand heaped caskets were seen in another place, also crystal, bronze and alabaster vases filled with rubies, topazes, sapphires and every gem known to man, with many not found on our planet and which sparkled in what seemed living fires of red, green, blue, orange and purple.

Still another part of the hall was filled with armor inlaid with precious metals and blazing with gems. Here also were goblets, cups, vases, lamps, candelabra and ten thousand other vessels and articles in the precious metals, all of the finest workmanship of both gods and men.

At sight of all these riches Dives literally gasped. He was so overcome by the vast and dazzling display that he was obliged to lean for support against one of the tall golden pillars of a great gallery that ran down one side of the hall, and there he stood staring in open-mouthed wonder. He was almost paralyzed.

Suddenly Plutus stood before us, seemingly coming from nowhere. In appearance he was a handsome youth and his eyes were full and sparkling, giving no hint of blindness; but he had the sad serious face and the listening attitude characteristic of the blind. He carried in his right hand a cornucopia that overflowed gems in a brilliant, rippling shower.

Dives was perceptibly awed, though the master of all the surrounding wealth was in appearance but little more than a child. He cleared his throat, gasped and hemmed, and at last in a puny and tremulous voice introduced himself as the shade of the "Honorable Magnificus Auriferous Dives, an ex-Senator of the United States of America, who has but lately arrived in these realms, your Majesty."

Plutus in a calm, even, business-like tone said that Dives was the first United States Senator who had ever to his knowledge visited that region, that nearly all went directly through by the straightest road to the Christian hell.

"Your Majesty would say to Heaven," Dives hastened to suggest.

"No," said Plutus. "Mercury, who often in his prying way, extends his flight to regions over the Christian side of the Phlegethon,[4] says he has observed that the majority bearing the title you have mentioned are quite unceremoniously tumbled into the dominions of Satan."

Dives hastened to change the subject by saying: "I observe, your Majesty, that silver constitutes the great bulk of your store of wealth."

"Aye, thou sayest right; silver is the money of the many."

"If I may be permitted to express my opinion, your Highness," said Dives, "gold is the only metal that is worthy of being coined into and dignified with the name of money. When I was in Congress, in 1873, by Jove, do you know that by a deuced clever little trick we actually demonetized silver!"[5]

"There didst thou act the part of a mere thief and scoundrel—a robber of the greater part of thy fellow men!" cried Plutus. "Thou didst outlaw the money of the many to double the value of that of the few. Silver was not demonetized by thee and thy kind because it had lost value as compared with gold, but that thou and thy tribe of usurers wished by outlawing that metal to give to the gold in your hands double its former purchasing power and thus place a yoke on the necks of all the millions of laboring poor—also to add to the weight of the yoke already borne by all men who were in debt. I find thee a mere robber. Silver is the coin I most delight to distribute, for it goes into the hands of the poor and needy; and thou who hast for years labored to reduce my beneficence by one-half, and thus defeat my intentions—thou hast the face to pass out of the direct road to the hell prepared for thee to beard me in my own house! I was made blind by great Jove in order that I might not bestow my treasures on the righteous alone, and but for that thou wouldst have been on earth the poorest among the poor. Get thee hence! I will not endure the presence of one of those who were instrumental in defeating my bounty, thus causing ceaseless wails to come to me from every civilized land on the face of the earth—hence with thee to hell!"

As we took our departure Dives said: "A deuced bitter little fellow that, by Jove! Has no more notion of political economy or financial strategy than a sucking babe!"

Notes

1. De Quille based his depiction of Plutus on some unusual representations of the god. Plutus is represented as a blind child in Aristophanes's *The Plutus*. He was also represented as a child on the bosom of Peace on a famous statue in Athens, symbolizing that Peace brings wealth. Plutus was included among the deities of the underworld to typify that riches are extracted from the earth.

2. See *Luke* 2:40–49.

3. Harun al-Rashid, a famous caliph of Baghdad, is mentioned in *The Arabian Nights*.

4. Phlegethon was a river of fire in Hades. Dante treats it as a place of torment.

5. De Quille chose to believe with other free silverites that the coinage law of 1873 (see "Introduction," p. 32) was an act of skullduggery. This was, and remains, an unfounded accusation. The coinage act was passed without opposition. Authorization was not given for the coinage of silver dollars because silver was selling at a higher price than the legal ratio of 16 units of silver to 1 of gold. It was not known in 1873 that silver prices would shortly drop.

Chapter VII.
The Elysian Fields—Diana and her Nymphs—Games of the Gods—Dives and Diogenes—"Asphodel Meadows"—Tartarus.

The region in which we had thus far been wandering still retained much of that gloom which characterized the whole of Hades during the entire reign of Erebus, its ancient primeval ruler, and the first part of the reign of Pluto, its present monarch. In the old early days the shades of the dead led a very dreary life. They were constantly in a dreamy semi-conscious state from which they could only be aroused by drinking the blood of sacrifices offered by friends in the upper world. The draughts of fresh, warm blood which they thus occasionally received endowed them for a brief period with all their former vigor, both mental and physical. So gloomy was this existence that Achilles assured Ulysses that he would "rather be the poorest day-laborer on earth than reign supreme in the realms of the dead."[1]

But times are now very different in Hades; indeed it is a very comfortable and cheerful sort of place. Commiserating the sad condition of the shades, Pluto eventually gave them as food and drink ambrosia and nectar, which serve the same purpose as the blood of sacrificed rams and oxen of former times, and to feast on which the shades rushed like swine; and in such herds that on one memorable occasion Ulysses was forced to draw his sword and drive them back. Pluto also lighted up several parts of his dominions, thus giving all the deserving shades a heaven filled with all the delights that could be imagined or desired by pagan spirits. It was toward these regions of light and joy that we now bent our steps.

Soon we reached much such a region as that into which we entered on crossing the Styx. No sooner had we come to the first of the beautiful groves and glades than Diana, with bow and quiver, and attended by a train of nymphs of the woods and springs swept along. The goddess was a full head taller than the tallest of her nymphs and all passed "as moon and stars glance along the clouded heaven, when winds are blowing strong."

"A deuced fine girl, that!" cried Dives—"I'm glad we've got out of these infernally dark regions into a place where a gentleman is likely to be treated as a gentleman. I must say that Plutus and the whole lot we've left behind are not much better than that damnable three-headed dog!"

Passing the golden palace—half in shade and half in light—where Aides and Persephone held their kindly court, we soon reached the Elysian Fields. This we found to be a truly blissful region. The air was fragrant, transparent rills sparkled through meadows that were sown with flowers of a thousand hues, and golden and starry-winged birds sang in all the groves:—

> "Here dance the Muses; and the Queen of Love
> Oft guides her golden car through this enchanting
> plain."

As we stood gazing upon the beauties of the place a troupe of shades of Grecian maidens passed us, singing as they danced along:—

> "Let us hasten, let us fly,
> When the roses bloom and blow.
> Heirs of immortality,
> Segregated, safe, and pure,
> Easy, sorrowless, secure,
> Since our earthly course is run
> We behold a brighter sun,
> Holy lives—a holy vow—
> Such rewards await us now."

We found the Elysian Fields thronged with happy shades engaged in those games and occupations in which they had delighted when on earth. Here the warrior found his horses, chariots, and arms; the musician his lyre, and the hunter his bow and quiver. In places we saw phalanxes charging in mimic fray and castles beseiged and defended. Arriving at a place—a sort of forum—where orators were disputing, we paused a while to listen. As we were turning away we saw reposing beneath a tree an old man, in whom I recognized Diogenes. He was listening with a look of mingled amusement and cynicism to the harangues of the orators, his ragged old mantle spread beside him.

Dives cast a contemptuous glance at the old man and in a disdainful tone said: "What beastly old tramp have we here?"

This roused the ire of the aged cynic. He turned a flashing eye upon Dives, the first notice he had given him, then—

> "Dreamer," he cried, "of streams that flowed with gold,
> My higher dignity in Hades behold!
> For all I had on earth this nether sphere
> Receives with me—but *thou* hast nothing here."

Along the borders of the Elysian Fields flowed Lethe, that gentle silent stream to drink whose waters brings utter forgetfulness of all former events—even of the joy of Elysium.

At no great distance beyond Lethe we came to the "Asphodel Meadows,"[2] the herding place of shades of innocuous mortals whose lives were distinguished by neither good nor bad actions. Here all the shades seemed moving about in a dreamy, listless way jabbering monotonously. The place appeared to be an asylum for all the idiots.

Adjoining the Asphodel Meadows we found the "Al Araf" of the Mahometans.[3] The two places were separated by nothing more substantial than a low hedge. Al Araf is situated on a long narrow promontory on one side of which is the Paradise and on the other the Jehennam of all followers of the Prophet. The infants, idiots and moral ciphers of Al Araf are allowed to converse freely with both the blessed and the cursed: to the former this region appears a hell; to the latter like heaven.

Giving to these places a mere passing glance we pursued our way down "sorrowful Acheron" to where it united with the waters of Cocytus, river of lamentation, and thence to Phlegethon—well called "Pyriphlegethon," as it is a river of flame.[4] Passing downward along this fiery flood, no means of crossing which was seen, we were startled at beholding a dark, whirling cloud approaching from which issued terrifying sounds.

Greatly alarmed, we stepped aside from the path we had been pursuing, and no sooner had we done so than a woman of gigantic stature appeared, thundering along on a great black horse. Her hair was formed of snakes, and her eyes glowed like living coals. So inky black was the cloud by which she was enveloped that naught but herself and steed could be seen. Out of the cloud came weird shrieks and yells mingling with the baying and howling of a great pack of dogs. It was Hecate[5] passing from Tartartus to the palace of Aides, or to the tribunal of Minos, and the very ground rocked as she swept along. Terrible as appeared this last of the titans in her visit to Tartarus, she takes on a beautiful form in Elysium and on earth, for she has rule in all these places. I recognized the goddess by her sword and torch, but knowing her greatness and justice, as well as benevolence, I felt no fear of her, though she appeared in her most terrible form, and notwithstanding the bad name that has been given her.

Dives was sure that the awful being was the devil, "out masquerading in his wife's clothes," and said to me in a husky voice: "I'm deucedly afraid that after all we'll be snapped up before we find a way out of this region of brimstone and smoke. It was rather fine up there in the Elysian Fields, but we are going from bad to worse—first into the idiot asylums of all nations and now, do you know, I think we are not far from the edge of the real burning hell they call Tartarus."

A turn of the fiery river brought us in sight of a tremendous tower or castle built of blocks of black basalt. It was the judgement hall of Rhadamanthus, the terrible judge who decides the punishment due to each shade found guilty and sent to him from the tribunal of his brother Minos, and turns them over to the Furies, who drive them with whips of living snakes to the great gate of Tartarus, and there tumble them in.

There seemed little doing at the court of Rhadamanthus, there being in these times few Greeks of the ancient faith to be operated upon. The Furies were loafing about the hall with sleeves rolled up and whips in their hands, looking like so many washerwomen in the sulks. Peeping into the judgement hall we saw old Rhadamanthus sitting as motionless upon his seat as though petrified. His white beard had grown so long that it flowed over and down the front of his black marble throne of judgement like a white veil. He seemed more a statue than thing of life, yet out of the face of a mummy looked eyes of fire.

Dives said he was mighty glad we would have good Christian judges to deal with, and not such "beastly and malevolent old heathen semi-devils" as we had seen. We walked out to the end of a pier that reached out over an abyss into which the flaming river Phlegethon poured with the thunder of a thousand Niagaras—poured blazing and hissing into Tartarus—Tartarus, "as far below as the stars are above the earth."

Deep as was the pit, and unfathomable by the eye, there arose to our ears a veritable pandemonium of shrieks and yells. There the two vultures tear at the liver of Tityus; there Tantalus hungers and thirsts up to his chin in water and with fruits so near that he can touch them with the tips of his fingers; there Sisyphus still heaves and strains at rolling the great stone up the steep, Ixion revolves on his wheel, and the Danaïdes strive to carry water in sieves.[6]

As we stood on the pier looking into depths so profound that all the floods of fiery Phlegethon could not light them up, I regaled Dives with a full account of the manner in which all these ladies and gentlemen were amusing themselves in the region below. He said it was no "civilized hell," but I reminded him that below our hell proper was a place much the same as Tartarus, known as "Fiddler's Green."[7]

As I by no means liked the place myself, I now proposed to return to the point where the Acheron joins the Cocytus and seek means of crossing the latter stream. I could still at times—particularly when lost in doubts and troubled with fears—see blazing afar a great light that sent up such beams and lances as on earth we see wavering above the boreal regions. Dives, who could see nothing, stoutly maintained that I imagined the light, still he was willing to follow where I led the way.

I told him that up at the Mahomedan Jehennam there was a bridge over the Phlegethon known as Al Serat, but it was not wider than the edge of a scimiter; that though the truly good cross in safety the bad invariably tumble off into the fiery flood. Dives said he would have nothing to do with the "blasted bridge," unless he might be allowed to "ride it upon a well-padded saddle."

Notes

1. See *The Odyssey*, Book 11.
2. The asphodel was said to be a flower that grew in the Elysian Fields.
3. In Islamic legend, "Al Araf" (i.e., the wall) is a narrow wall between Heaven and Hell (Jehennam) where dwell the dead who are neither good nor evil. De Quille appears to be using the original meaning of the term, and not the new one Poe created in his poem, "Al Aaraaf."
4. Acheron, Cocytus, Phlegethon (or Pyriphlegethon), Styx, and Lethe are all rivers of Hades. Dante included the first four in the *Inferno* and Lethe in the *Purgatorio*.
5. Hecate, mentioned in Hesiod's *Theogony*, Aristophanes's *Plutus*, and Virgil's *Aeneid*, was a patroness of witches. Some of the detail of this passage may have been invented by De Quille.
6. Tartarus was that part of the classical world where evil was punished. Virgil locates Tityus, Tantalus, Sisyphus, and Ixion there in the *Aeneid*, Book VI. He does not specifically mention the Danaides, although Greek legend relegated them to Tartarus.
7. Normally, Fiddler's Green is thought of as an Elysian Fields of sailors and vagabond craftsmen. De Quille's conception of it appears to be his own.

Chapter VIII.
The Bridge Bifrost—Heimdall the Sentinel—Valhalla—A Battle of the Happy Warriors—The Walkyries—House of Odin—Hela.

I then bethought me of the bridge called Bifrost, reaching over to Asgard, the Heaven of the Teutonic nations, which I believed to span the Acheron at a point just below the confluence of the stream and the Cocytus. Proceeding thither our hearts were gladdened by the sight of an immense bridge, resplendent with all the colors of the rainbow. Dives was delighted and said: "By Jove, I shall always hereafter have a better opinion of the Dutch."[1]

The bridge was a noble arch with high parapets of solid brass, surmounted with statues of silver and gold. Over the entrance was inscribed in letters formed of flashing gems the two words—"Gluck Auf!"[2]

Before the bridge stood Heimdall, sentinel of the gods, with his horse. Heimdall "sleeps less than a bird, sees even in sleep, can hear the grass grow, and even the wool on a lamb's back." At our approach he sounded his great horn till the sky seemed ready to fall with its thunderous peals and blasts. Then taking up his sword, shield and battle-ax he placed himself on guard and began patrolling to and fro across the entrance.

At sight of this formidable sentinel Dives was much troubled until I explained to him that all was one in mere courtesy; that the horn was blown to notify the gods in Asgard and Valhalla of the approach of visitors, that the armor was assumed in order to give us a formal reception, and that to be permitted to pass we had but to say we were pilgrims come to drink of Mimir's well, the fountain of all wisdom rising at the root of the celestial ash.[3]

Going boldly up to the guardian of the bridge, I informed him that we were pilgrims from the Midgard, come to pay our respects to the All-Fader and drink of the well of Mimir.

Stepping aside and pointing across the bridge, Heimdall told us to proceed on our way.

"A very good sort of fellow," said Dives after we had passed.

"Yes," said I, "it is doubtless owing to his being so well born. He is the son of nine virgins, all sisters. He is a sort of Scandinavian Gabriel, for at the end of the world he will sound the trumpet. Then all the gods will wake, the sons of Muspell will then march against them with fire, with the wolf Fenris and the great serpent Jormungander, and in the fray the world will be consumed in flames.[4] Heimdall has a great deal on his mind."

As I spake Heimdall began singing:

> "Lauterbach hab' i mein' Strumpf verlorn,
> Ohne Strumpf geh' i not hoam,
> Geh' i halt weider auf Lauterbach,
> Kauf' mir an Strumpf zu den oan.
> Tillee leari, oiko, hi oiko, hi oiko!
> Z'Lauterbach hab' i nein Herz verlorn,
> Ohne Herz Kann i not leb'n—"[5]

Until we were far on our way over the bridge the—"Tillee leari, oiko, hi oiko" of the guardian god continued to reach our ears.

"By Jove," said Dives, "his mind does seem to be deucedly oppressed with the cares of his office!"

Having crossed the bridge, we found before us the plain of Ida and the city of Asgard. Before the city stood the great "house of joy" known as Gladsheim, with about it Glasur, the grove whose trees bear leaves of silver and gold. Strolling near to Gladsheim, we heard thousands of voices singing, and caught the words.—

> "Deutschland, Deutschland, uber Alles,
> Uber Alles in der Welt!"[6]

"Good Lord," cried Dives, "we've struck a Dutch camp meeting!"

Near Gladsheim stood the vast hall known as Valhalla, so high that the wolf hung out from its main tower as the symbol of war, looked no bigger than a rat. This great war hall has 540 doors, through each of which 800 men may march out abreast. Every morning at the crowing of the cock the inmates seize their arms and rushing out fight furiously with each other till noon, when all wounds are healed and the happy warriors return to a feast in the hall, with Odin, the All-Fader, heading the table.

One of these daily battles was raging in the plain of Ida at the time of our visit, and the "Walkyries," or battle-maidens, in brilliant armor and all ablaze with gold and jewels were dashing through the air aloft in troops, all on steeds made fierce as tigers by the smell of blood. The light from their lances illuminated the air in whatever place they rode. While some thus hovered over the field of battle others, dismounted from their steeds, stood on a hill and poured forth a battle-song so wild and fierce that its notes were heard above the thunder and clash of the conflict in the plain below.

At Odin's private residence, Einherian,[7] we saw his two black ravens, Huginn (thought) and Muninn (memory), which fly forth daily to gather all that is being done in the world. Often they are to be seen sitting on Odin's shoulders, each having possession of an ear. Here we also saw the All-Fader's steed, Sleipner, the eight-legged gray horse which carried his master over seas as well as land; his spear, Gungner, which never fails to hit the mark aimed at; his ring, Draupner, which every ninth night drops eight other rings of equal value, and also saw his two wolves, Geri and Freki. We saw besides the sacred ash, monster serpents, winged dogs and a thousand other wonders.

In leaving the "Dutch Heaven," as Dives persisted in calling it, we had to be on our guard against taking the Hel-way, a dangerous road that leads downward, through a valley where each blade of grass is a sword, and to the north to Helheim, the place of residence of the infernal goddess Hela. Hela is not a personage it is desirable to visit, as she binds all she receives with chains that cannot be broken. She holds the keys of nine hells, each lower than the other. The lowest is called Anguish and it is into this ninth hell that she puts the worst of her subjects. The threshold of this place is Precipice, the table Famine, the waiters Slowness and Delay, and the bed Care. Hela rides a horse with only three legs, yet is swifter than the wind, and has an agreeable brother in the form of a demon wolf, not to mention a terrible dog that stands guard at Helgate.

Dives was much afraid of wandering away into the dominions of Mrs. Hela. He said to be at the mercy of a male devil would be bad enough.

Notes

1. "Dutch" (as in Pennsylvania Dutch) is a popular corruption of the German word "Deutsch"—meaning "German." Here it is loosely extended to all Teutonic, including Scandinavian, peoples.

2. "Gluck auf!" is a German miners' term for "Good Luck!"

3. One of the three roots of Yggdrasill, the eternal ash tree, touches the well of Mimir, whose waters are a source of wisdom. Odin, the All-Father, gave one eye for a single drink from it. The notion that pilgrims from the Midgard (earth) were free to approach the well appears to be an invention of De Quille.

4. Lazarus here briefly sums up the Norse legend of Ragnarok, the end of the gods and the world.

5. Heimdall's song is a traditional folk melody from Bavaria, sung in Bavarian dialect. An approximate translation follows:

> I have lost my stocking in Lauterbach,
> Without a stocking I go not home,

So I will go back to Lauterbach again,
And buy myself another stocking like the one I have.
Tillee leari, oiko, hi oiko, hi oiko!
In Lauterbach I lost my heart,
Without a heart I cannot live—

De Quille seems to have considered Germans and Scandinavians interchangeable and, not knowing any Scandinavian songs, incongruously used one that he might have learned from German miners in Virginia City.

6. Another incongruous use of a German song for Norse gods.

Germany, Germany, over all,
Over everything in the World!

These lines were from a patriotic poem by Hoffman von Fallersleben. After Haydn put it to music, it became an unofficial German anthem in the nineteenth century.

7. The Einherjar were the slain heroes brought to Valhalla by the Valkyries. De Quille may have renamed Valhalla for these warriors.

Chapter IX.
Utgard Giants and Pigmies—The Sprite of the Juniper-tree— The Chief of the Gnomes and Kobolds—A Subterranean Journey.

In order to get out of the Scandinavian heaven we had first to cross Ida's plain through Asgard to Midgard (the middle ward), thence to Utgard (the outer ward). The first is easy enough, but Utgard is a circle of rocks; among which dwell Utgard-Loki and many terrible giants, or "joten," therefore the rocky region is also known as Jotenheim—the home of the giants. This was a perilous place through which to pass. When we reached the borders of this outlying dangerous region and saw before us a circle of precipitous hills on the summit of which huge castellated racks towered so thickly that only narrow alleys and paths were to be seen between them, we halted and sat down beneath a juniper-tree to consider what course to pursue. Among the lower rocks, in great commotion, we could see the giants moving about, both male and female, and all of Brobdingnagian stature, while on the crest of the ridge above them pinnacles of rock towered aloft until almost lost in the general purple haze of the upper air.

While we were discussing the advisability of turning back, a small musical voice attracted our attention. This voice seemed to come from the tree under which we were seated, but we could see no living thing near us. We were then informed that we were being addressed by the sprite natural to the tree beneath which we sat.

"How can that be?" asked Dives—"It is something new to learn that trees are creatures—that they have a sort of life."

I then explained to him that when the gods of Asgard took counsel and determined to create new beings with which to people the universe, their first attempt did not result in the production of human beings. When the gods saw that the dead body of Ymir (of which the earth was formed) was filled with little maggot-like creatures they gave them human forms and understanding. The beings thus formed became dwarfs and sprites, and took up their abodes in the bowels of the earth, in rocks, trees, plants and flowers. Seeing this result of the first attempt, and wishing to people the surface of the earth, Odin and two companions went into the Midgard region, where they found the trees Ask (ash) and Embla (elm) and of them created man and woman; and from this pair came the whole human race.

Again we heard the voice of the sprite of our tree. "I know what you desire and what you fear," said the spirit, "and I will send a message to those who can guide and assist you." The sprite then whispered a message to the grass and flowers and they to the plants and trees on the plain until at last the words reached the elves dwelling in the caves and amid the rocks of the earth.

These pigmies of the rocks are constantly at war with the giants, and often get the better of them by undermining the cliffs of the mountains constituting the Jotenheim, causing them to fall or crash together and crush the huge monsters. The message sent by the sprite was a request that an elf of the rocks be sent to guide two shades from the upper world through the secret passage ways beneath the encircling mountains of the joten to the peaceful realms beyond. This region beyond the rocks of the giants was filled, we were told by the sprite of the juniper-tree, with the shades of creatures that had never been endowed with life in any sphere in the universe—the shades of things as unsubstantial as dreams, yet far better known on the earth than the majority of its real human inhabitants. Through the territory of these shades we might pass unquestioned and unharmed.

Soon the novel style of telegraphy adopted by our sprite of the tree brought from the zone of rocks an elf in the form of a mountain rat. We followed his ratship to a deep rift near at hand at the plain, when he at once assumed his natural form. To our surprise we saw before us an agile little man about two feet in height, whose complexion was of the color of granite—speckled with black and flecked with red. He was jauntily dressed in a close-fitting jacket of green, wore black knee-breeches, orange stockings, shoes of a burnt-sienna hue; and a scarlet cap with a black feather standing straight up in front. The little fellow was armed with a sort of spring gun which fired barbed needles so swiftly that they became red-hot in their flight, as he showed us. Apparently the needle received a charge of electricity at the instant it took its flight, as behind the spiral spring of the weapon was that which appeared to be an electrical chamber. These guns the pigmies used against their giant foes by firing up through crevices in the rocks. Daily from thousands of crevices red-hot needles were shot up into the bulky bodies of the giants. Thus were the jotens of Jotenheim made unhappy.

Being unable to penetrate into the clefts and fissures where the elves ran about like weasels, the Gargantuan Utgarders in their rage and pain would at times grasp the tops of tall cliffs and by alternately pulling and pushing would cause an awful grinding and crashing at their roots, far down in the interior of the mountain, often pulverizing whole swarms of

elves in the subterranean chambers of the mountains. To avenge themselves the elves would then undermine the rocky walls in places where
the joten had alley-ways, and by suddenly knocking out tens of
thousands of props would cause parallel lines of cliffs to snap together,
squeezing flat whole processions of the great lumbering Utgarders, im-
prisoning them for ages.

All these things were told us by our guide as we passed along toward
the towering ridge of rocks. He was a "jarl" and a chieftain of great
prowess and high renown among his people. The cleft we were following
ended in a narrow fissure that penetrated the rocks that formed the base
of the mountain of the Utgard. Through this fissure we squeezed and
soon found ourselves in a labyrinth of subterranean passages. The place
swarmed with elves, gnomes and pigmies as a rabbit warren swarms with
rabbits.

Our guide was greatly pleased when his people informed him that
they had just inflicted severe punishment upon the giants in a heavy
skirmish that had occurred. Thus was the commotion we had witnessed
among the Jotenheimers when we first sighted their abode accounted for.
A score of red-hot needles, each as long as a good-wife's knitting-needle,
planted in the fat rump of a joten could but tend to render him temporari-
ly lively.

There appeared to be millions of sprites of the rocks, elves, gnomes,
kobolds and pigmies of every known breed in the honeycombed heart of
the mountain. Thus far the little people seemed in every way to have the
advantage in their battles with their bulky antagonists. The only means of
offensive warfare possessed by the joten, of which the pigmies stood in
dread, was that of grasping and churning the tall tower-like rocks. When
a host of the giants planted themselves on each side of a great cliff and
began swaying it back and forth the commotion at its roots, deep in the
bowels of the mountain, was such that vast areas of rock were ground to
powder and thousands of chambers, passages and caverns annihilated.
Fortunately for the little people the joten were not aware of the damage
they did and they seldom resorted to rocking the peaks—only when
greatly exasperated by the sting of myriads of fiery arrows and quite at
their wit's end.

Luckily for us the giants refrained from churning the rocks while we
were in and passing through the broad base of the Utgard mountain
chain, and after a long and winding journey through many grand
passages, arched chambers and vast natural caverns, preceded and followed by thousands of pigmy torch-bearers, we at last emerged into the
open through a narrow fissure at the head of a beautiful little glen. There,
with many thanks, we took our leave of our Lilliputian jarl, who in his
proper form would not move a single step into the open country.

Chapter X.
The Limbo of Myth and Fiction—Don Quixote—Robinson Crusoe—Robin Hood and Other Celebrities.

At the foot of the glen ran a small brook beyond which lay a picturesque region of undulating plains, rounded hills, ranges of rocky mountains, and many lakes and streams both large and small. Castles of great size, and of a thousand picturesque and grotesque styles of architecture, were seen crowning the hills, with here and there walls and fortresses of every kind known in the art of war. Also there were seen in the valley, about the lakes and along the streams, palaces, cottages, lodges and bowers in bewildering and endless variety. Inhabitants in abundance were everywhere visible. They were seen moving in a thousand different directions. They were on foot, on horseback, in carriages and even traveled by railroad and steamboat. The dresses of the people, seen at the distance from which we were looking down upon the country, appeared to be of all the colors of the rainbow—the whole scene was decidely kaleidoscopic.

After we had gazed for some moments upon the scene I have outlined, Dives heaved a huge sigh of relief, and turning to me he cried: "Again I live! I feel my soul revive within me! By Jove, don't you know, this is something like a heaven! It is a place in which a gentleman and a Christian may take some comfort; for, see, it has railroads and steamboats—no doubt we shall also find the telegraph, telephone, electric lights and all the modern improvements. It must be that we have at last got to heaven. 'Pon honor it looks just like England! I even fancy that I know some of those castles. I do not much doubt that a leading member of the English nobility may here be provided with a facsimile of the castle he was obliged to leave behind. It would be deuced fine, now, were I to find snugly established here in heaven some of my old English friends—the Earl of Goldpot, or the Duke of Damtherabble![1] Well, at all events I am glad to see that the place is civilized—that it is a heaven fit for modern Christians. But, by the way, we must now soon reach a place where a passport or something of the kind will be demanded. Let me see—How much did I say I gave for a hospital for disabled cats? You see our trip through all the hells and heavens, with our dive under that rotten old mountain, where all those beastly giants were dancing Highland flings over our heads, has quite put me out. I've run over the list of my bequests scores of times, but I always seem to miss something."

"Perhaps," suggested I, "it is what you gave to the family of poor Tim Smith when he was chewed up in your paper-pulp factory?"

"No; no, it was no such trifling affair as that. I never bothered about Smith, further than to get in his place a man who had sense enough to keep out of the machinery—but, yes, I did tell some of my men that I'd like them to take their washing to Mrs. Smith, as she had a large family to support. But what I am trying to think of is a matter of importance—a matter of a hundred thousand or more."

And as we took our way down the glen Dives was muttering over his list of bequests, I could catch fragments of said list as follows: "Baptist Church, $250,000; Catholic Church, $500,000; Methodist Mission, $200,000," etc.

So he ran on and did not raise his eyes from the ground until we had arrived at the brook flowing across the foot of the glen, and then was not aroused until I uttered an exclamation of surprise. And well might I be surprised and even startled, for cantering along down the opposite bank of the brook rode Don Quixote, mounted upon his famous Rosinante, while some distance in the rear came laboring along Sancho Panza, seated upon his darling burro, Dapple. I recognized the pair instantly.

"Good Lord!" cried Dives—"What kind of a ragamuffin old duffer is that on the hoss?" and he looked quite disgusted and chap-fallen.

"A famous knight of the olden times," said I.

"What! Not St. George that slew the dragon?" cried Dives, brightening somewhat.

"No, this is the Knight of the Sorrowful Countenance—one who performed a thousand feats of valor in Spain on mountain and plain—a man so fierce that even the king of beasts turned tail beneath the fire of his eagle eye. Look, he is preparing to charge—he is placing his lance in rest!"

"I see no other knight for him to charge," said Dives.

"Look!" cried I, as the old knight spurred his steed and set out at a sort of rickety gallop toward a windmill, distant some two hundred yards. As the knight charged the great fans sent both man and steed sprawling to grass.

"By Jove!" cried Dives, "I think I've read or heard of that crazy old fool somewhere."

Crossing the brook upon a little rustic bridge, we plunged boldly into the valley that lay before us. We were quite unnoticed, for the thousands about us were all clapping their hands and shouting—were applauding Don Quixote in his great windmill act.

We had gone only a little way before, in a sort of circular hollow, we saw a pond of water about two hundred feet in diameter with a little rocky island in the center. On the summit of the island stood a shaggy-haired, long-bearded man clad in goat skins. He held over his head an umbrella of skins and feathers, and seemed talking to a parrot perched on his shoulder, while a kid or two gamboled near.

"Behold!" cried I, "Robinson Crusoe on the island of Juan Fernandez!"[2]

"I read something about him when I was a boy," said Dives, "but don't remember of his doing anything to entitle him to a place in heaven."

Just at this moment there was a great blowing of horns and yelping of dogs and the "Wild Huntsman" sped by.[3]

Proceeding onward we entered the edge of a little wood when we encountered Robin Hood, Little John, Friar Tuck, and Maid Marian. Bold Robin was in the lead, with bow in hand; giant Little John marched at his heels, and next came Friar Tuck in his russet habit, a red corded girdle with gold tassel about his Falstaffian waist, red stockings on his legs and a wallet on his back. Such was Tuck—

"The merry friar, which many a sermon made,
In praise of Robin Hood, his outlaws, and their trade."

Maid Marian, a wild-eyed witch, also carried a bow, like a second Diana. She danced along at the heels of Tuck, and loudly laughed at some holy jest that the friar threw at her over his shoulder. Thus merrily marching, all disappeared in the green wood we were passing.

All this time Dives had been staring wildly about, his face wearing a most puzzled expression. Just as he had attained this condition of nervous uncertainty with regard to the status of the place, the Pied Piper of Hamelin came marching by, followed by some three hundred fascinated children, who, pale-faced and wild-eyed, stared at the visage of the pipe-playing devil—

"To blow the pipe his lips he wrinkled,
And green and blue his sharp eyes twinkled."

When this strange sight had passed before his eyes Dives cried out in alarm: "What sort of Bedlam place have we stumbled into here, with its processions and masquerades? If it is heaven we must have struck it on a holiday."

As Dives thus gave vent to his vexation, a dapper little gentleman in knee-breeches and cocked-hat, who had for some time been lingering near, stepped up to him and bowing politely said: "Pray, sir, excuse me for making so bold as to introduce myself. I am Lemuel Gulliver, by birth of Nottinghamshire, England. I am that Gulliver whose travels in Lilliput,

Brobdingnag, Laputa, and the land of the Houyhnhnms have, I believe, made some noise in the upper world. As I perceive you to be strangers here, I take pleasure in making known to you that this happy place is the 'Limbo of Myth and Fiction.' Here all personages, creatures and things born of the brains of men of genius have an actual existence. Here are not only personages of note, but here are also to be found all the castles, palaces, rose-embowered cottages, huts, caverns and the like of which you read in the chronicles of the race to which I belong. Yes, and here, at no great distance, you will find Lilliput and the other strange lands mentioned in the history of my travels. We have been thus favored and given an existence and a place in the universe for the reason that the supernatural powers that rule in these realms consider the children that are born of the brains of men of genius—of that soul which is immortal—as being more worthy of eternal existence than often are the children begotten of their mere earthly and perishable bodies. Here, beings that were mere intangible dreams to you of the upper world are bodied forth and given a degree of substantiality little different from that which you now possess in your present capacity of shades of bodies left behind in the tomb."

Notes

1. In addition to his other sins, Dives has now revealed himself to be something of an Anglophile. De Quille placed heavy blame on England for promoting the gold standard.

2. Juan Fernandez is an island off the coast of Chile that supposedly suggested the setting for the one Defoe described in *Robinson Crusoe*.

3. The "Wild Huntsman" is the first of a series of characters from fairy tales, legends, and Mother Goose stories that appear in the Limbo of Myth and Fiction. The "Wild Huntsman" is the subject of a number of German folk tales centering about a hunter who was compelled to hunt ceaselessly.

Chapter XI.
Gulliver as a Guide—Sindbad—Ancient Mariner—Falstaff—Babes in the Wood—Mother Goose—The Seven Sleepers, Etc. Etc.

Of this about all that Dives understood, or cared to understand, was that the speaker was English, and that he was born in Nottingham. He at once grasped the hand of the demi-shade and cried: "By Jove! Mr. Gulliver, I'm deuced glad to see you, to be sure! I shall be glad to make your acquaintance, sir. Ah, well do I remember old Nottingham! Well do I remember the vale of the Trent, and the old castle above your town—that castle of the days of William the Conqueror—William with whom my own family, the Diveses, came to 'Merrie England'—also the pleasant waters and meadow of the river Leen, and a thousand other beautiful places. By Jove, Mr. Gulliver, do you know, I can see it all now, in my mind's eye!"

Dives and Gulliver then linked arms and we all moved on together; Gulliver trying to persuade Dives to take a little run with him to the land of Lilliput. Gulliver said they would make up a little party—his old friend Baron Munchausen would be glad to make one of the party, and he would be found a very truthful and entertaining gentleman.[1]

As we were pleasantly strolling along a sailor-looking man ran panting past, having on his back a little old man whose wrinkled face looked like that of an ape. The legs of the little man were wound tightly about the neck of the other, while across his forehead were clasped his long claw-like hands. The eyes of the wrinkled old creature were of a venomous green, and he hissed wrathfully as he spurred his bearer's breast with his long bony heels.

"Poor Sindbad!" cried Mr. Gulliver, "he cannot find in all these realms any kind of beverage possessed of sufficient body to make his execrable old rider drunk."[2]

Seeing a man seated on a bench under a tree by the wayside, I asked him what he did there all alone. "My good sir," said he, "I am waiting for something to turn up."[3]

Passing on we presently saw two men in a little vale at work upon a series of miniature fortifications. They were so deeply absorbed in their occupation as to be oblivious of our presence. They had models of towns and castles, with surrounding walls and moats; forts, drawbridges and earthworks upon which they were mounting little cannon. They then placed a toy church in a town hard by. The younger of the pair proposed that they hang bells in the tower of the church.

"Nay, Trim," said the elder, a soldierly looking man with a slight limp, "nay, Trim, let the metal be cast into cannon."[4]

A moment later, as we passed on, a wild-eyed man in the dress of a sailor, with a long gray beard and the countenance of a maniac, suddenly rose from a hedge, darted out among us. Planting himself in front of Dives and grasping him with his skinny hand, the queer old creature shrieked at him: "There was a ship!—"

"What fiend is this?" cried Dives, striving to shake off the old man's bony hand and looking horrified.

Still holding his grasp, the crack-brained stranger bent his face to that of Dives—to "hold him with his glittering eye"—and in a shrill voice screeched:—

> "The ship was cheered, the harbour cleared,
> Merrily did we drop
> Below the kirk, below the hill,
> Below the lighthouse tap."—

"Enough!" cried Gulliver, pushing the old man aside, "we all have heard thy ghastly tale," and as the baffled wretch crept back into the hedge to lie in wait for the next passer-by our guide quietly said: "The 'Ancient Mariner,' the man who killed the albatross. Poor old devil, he has been crazy ever since."

At a bend in the road we came upon a little tavern in front of which stood a man who was a "mountain of flesh," and with a companion with a flaming nose of monstrous size. The pair were wrangling with a vixenish looking woman, who stood in the inn door and shrilly cried: "Master Tisick, the deputy, but a day or two ago said to me, said he—'You are a good woman, and well thought on; therefore take heed what guests you receive. Receive,' says he, 'no swaggering companions.'"

Gulliver lifted his hat to the fat man, then turning to Dives said: "Sir John Falstaff, a very valiant warrior."

"Yes," said Dives, "I think I remember hearing that he killed Hotspur."

"Aye," that he did," said Gulliver, "but this is not his day for doing that act."[5]

Soon after passing Dame Quickly's tavern we saw approaching two men; one quite young. The young man wore a doublet with slashed sleeves, knee breeches and a cloak, the whole of blue velvet embroidered with gold. The elder of the pair was beyond middle age, wore a long black cloak, was a tall, meagre, pale man and had a very solemn appearance. As they passed us the old man was saying to his young companion: "But I intend to go a shorter way to work and spare thee the trouble of studying pharmacy, anatomy, botany and physic: know, my friend, all that is required is to bleed the patients and make them drink warm water. This is the secret of curing all distempers incident to man. Yes! that wonderful secret which I reveal to thee, and which nature, impenetrable to my brethren, hath not been able to hide from my researches, is contained in these two points, of plentiful bleeding and frequent draughts of water. I have nothing more to impart; thou now knowest physic to the very bottom."

As Dives and Gulliver gave no heed to the pair, I said nothing, but I recognized in them two very old friends.[6]

Leaving the main road we entered a region of low hills, groves, and little valleys. As we were passing through a bit of wood, Mr. Gulliver placed a finger on his lips and pointed to a little nook among some brambles. Looking in we there saw the dead bodies of the "Children of the Wood."

The children lay locked in each other's arms, their little faces sadly stained with berry juice. Hard by was perched a robin, and seeing that he was expected to do his duty the bird began to cover the bodies of the babes with leaves. As I gazed, I thought of the aged minstrel of whom it is written—

> "Then sad he sung 'The Children in the Wood.'
> (Ah! barbarous uncle, stained with infant blood!)
> How blackberries they plucked in deserts wild,
> And fearless at the glittering falchion smiled;
> Their little corpse the robin-redbreast found,
> And strewed with pious bill the leaves around."

Asking us to excuse his emotion, Gulliver wiped a tear from his eye, whereupon Dives gave me a wink and whispered in my ear that he had "seen the same thing in a puppet-show."[7]

On leaving the wood we came to a little hollow valley in which there was a tremendous gabbling, piping, clatter, and commotion. I at first thought we had come upon a pond in which were myriads of frogs, but Mr. Gulliver informed us that what we heard was merely a dress rehearsal that was being held by old "Mother Goose." Directing my gaze toward the upper end of the little hollow, I saw Mother Goose herself. She wore a filled cap of the size of an umbrella and was seated upon a sort of throne. By her side was an immense gray goose. The old lady's progeny filled all the little valley, and even its sides, as in an amphitheater. Each bantling was at work at its specialty. The old lady frequently applauded by clapping her hands, and as often as she did so the goose upreared its neck and shrieked so shrilly that single-handed it might have saved Rome.

We beat a hasty retreat from the place, but for a time seemed to have made a leap out of the frying-pan into the fire; for, almost immediately, we encountered "Jack the Giant Killer," "Jack and his Beanstalk," the "House that Jack Built," with all its inhabitants, and saw "Jack and Jill come tumbling down the hill."

Next we saw the "Sleeping Beauty," shut up in an enchanted castle of glass; "Cinderella," in her glass slippers; "Little Red Ridinghood" and the wolf, and also the castle of "Blue Beard."

Soon we got upon fairer and better ground, when we saw "Uncle Tom" and "Little Eva"[8]; "Uncle Remus" and "the little boy"[9]; and then "Little Nell"—the only Little Nell. "She was dead. No sleep so beautiful and calm, so free from trace of pain, so fair to look upon."[10] Even Dives dropped a tear.

Moving on we presently saw Peter Schlemihl, "the man without a shadow,"[11] and with him John Doe and Richard Roe, arm in arm. Behind these came at a sedate pace "Old Grimes," who "used to wear a long black coat all buttoned down before." Of this good old man it has been said—

> "He lived at peace with all mankind,
> In friendship he was true;
> His coat had pocket-holes behind,
> His pantaloons were blue."[12]

Passing into a more wild and rocky region, we came suddenly upon Epimenides, the Cretan poet. Epimenides is the man who went forth to find and fetch a sheep, and after sleeping 57 years continued his search, and was surprised to find when he got home that his younger brother was grown gray. Holding to the coat-tails of the Greek was Peter Klaus, the goatherd of Sittendorf, who going into the Kyffhaüser, got into a game of skittles with twelve silent personages, tasted of their wine and fell into a sleep that lasted twenty years; and holding to the coat-tails of Peter was old Rip Van Winkle. The procession was headed for the cave of the "Seven Sleepers of Ephesus," and the cave being hard by, we followed the pilgrim disciples and peeped into it. We found the "seven" sleeping as soundly as ever and snoring dreadfully. Their dog, who had been standing all the time, day and night, for ages without eating, drinking or sleeping, faithfully keeping guard, was so thin and weak that he was obliged to brace himself against the side of the cave before he dared so much as venture a growl.[13]

Mr. Gulliver informed us that the dog had given up barking some 200 years before, that kind of demonstration being a mere unprofitable vanity.

I observed that in gazing in upon the sleepers the Greek, Peter and Rip took off their hats.

Dives was disgusted. "A lot of fellows curled up like pigs in a sty," said he, "and all such beastly snorers!"

On leaving the cave of the "Seven Sleepers," I asked Mr. Gulliver if Grangousier, his son Gargantua, and his grandson, Pantagruel, inhabited that section; and if it were true that the latter combed his head with a comb 900 feet long and picked his teeth with the tusk of an elephant, and withal was a "bottomless pit of knowledge."[14]

"Gargantua is a man-mountain," said Mr. Gulliver, "and altogether they are a low, beastly set with whom we do not associate, therefore they loaf about the borders of this realm on the shores of Oceanus, that ever-flowing stream which encircles the universe. In no other place could there be found a room for such filthy lubbers."

It was easily to be seen that Mr. Gulliver was prejudiced in favor of his Brobdingnagians, therefore changing the subject I said: "I do not myself particularly admire the coarse brutes, but I would much like to see some of the famous knights of whose feats of arms all the world has heard. Such mirrors of chivalry, for instance, as Orlando Furioso, Amadis de Gaul, Astolpho, Don Ktrielüson of Greece, Rinaldo, Ogier the Dane, Sir Huon of Bordeaux, Montesinos of the cave, and Mambrino of the enchanted helmet.[15] Also, I would like to see some of the dragons, serpents, giants, and other monsters with which these valiant souls are wont to war."

"You are enthusiastic," said Gulliver, "and I would be much pleased to gratify your curiosity, but—but the truth is (here Mr. Gulliver colored slightly)—the truth is they are a high-flying set. Although we would willingly fraternize with them, and have made all kinds of friendly advances, they hold themselves aloof from us in a region over which they claim sole rule. They affect to look down upon us as mere parvenus—upstarts—personages of no pedigree. They are a haughty, supercilious tribe—as full of vanities as a dog is of fleas—all glitter, jingle, feathers, embroidery, strut and swagger. It is looked upon by their arrogant lordships as the height of presumption for any one to come among them who is not clad in steel from top to toe, mounted upon a gallant steed and followed by a big bull-headed squire. Yet not one among them dare stand before our champion, Don Quixote; even Furioso slinks out of sight when the redoubtable 'Knight of the Lions' makes his appearance."

Divining how matters stood from Gulliver's momently increasing bitterness, I said nothing more about the knights and turning to Dives called his attention to where, on one side of the way, William Tell was shooting the apple off his son's head, while on the other Pocahontas was diligently engaged in rescuing Captain John Smith's skull from her father's club.

We saw the castle of Miragarda and a score of other castles, abbeys, monasteries and old ruins, and still had ten thousand other things and personages to see, when Dives declared he felt that he already had a "gorge of Bedlam trash," and desired to be shown at once to the "Cave of Mammon", where was to be found "something solid."

At mention of old Mammon's den, I observed Mr. Gulliver scowl and shrug his shoulders. He excused himself from attending us farther, saying that pressing affairs in Lilliput required his attention, but he gave us minute directions for finding the cave, which he said was on the border of the "Limbus Fatuorum," or "Fool's Paradise," a place wherein dwell idiots and others of Earth's unaccountables. These persons not being responsible for their works while in the flesh are not punished in purgatory, neither can they be received into heaven, therefore have a paradise of their own.

Notes

1. Baron Munchausen was the title character of an extremely popular collection of tall tales first published in London in 1785. Gulliver appears naive about Munchausen's veracity.

2. The Old Man of the Sea is Sindbad's rider. From *The Arabian Nights*.

3. Mr. Micawber, from Dickens's *David Copperfield*.

4. Uncle Toby and his servant, Trim, from *Tristram Shandy*, by Laurence Sterne.

5. This scene featuring Sir John Falstaff and Dame Quickly is from *2 Henry IV*. II.iv. Neither Gulliver nor Dives appears to be very familiar with Shakespeare; Falstaff was not valiant, and he did not kill Hotspur.

6. The older man was Doctor Sangrado; the younger, Gil Blas. From chapter 20 of *Gil Blas* (1715), a famous French novel by Alain René Le Sage.

7. Sentimental stories, poems, and even puppet-show skits based on the tale of children murdered by a cruel uncle are standard items of children's literature.

8. Little Eva and the slave Uncle Tom are the main characters of Harriet Beecher Stowe's *Uncle Tom's Cabin* (1852).

9. The dialect animal stories of *Uncle Remus* (1880), by Joel Chandler Harris, are told to a little boy on a plantation by Uncle Remus, an old black retainer.

10. From the conclusion of *The Old Curiosity Shop*, by Dickens.

11. Peter Schlemihl was the main character in the romantic 1814 novel of the same name, by Adalbert von Chamisso.

12. Old Grimes is the title character of a popular children's poem by Albert Gorton Greene.

13. De Quille has listed four stories, from different cultures and different ages, all variations on the motif of characters who fall into an enchanted sleep and awake years or even centuries later. The most recent is Washington Irving's "Rip Van Winkle" (1819). A source for that was one of the German legends about the mystical Kyffhaüser mountain that was collected and published as "Peter Klaus the Goatherd." Preceding those stories were the famous medieval legends of Epimenides, which De Quille summarizes, and the "Seven Sleepers of Ephesus." This latter tale is about seven early Christians from Ephesus who

refused to obey an emperor's edict to sacrifice to Roman idols. They hid in a cave and slept for 360 years, until Ephesus became Christian. This grouping is particularly interesting as it reveals De Quille to be a student as well as a reader of folklore.

14. Allusions to *Gargantua* and *Pantagruel,* sixteenth century classics of humor by François Rabelais.

15. It is not clear how much De Quille knew about each of these chivalric heroes. It is possible but not probable that De Quille read Lodovico Ariosto's famous and influential heroic poem, *Orlando Furioso* (1532); it was available in translation. Most of the other characters' stories can be found summarized in Bulfinch's *Mythology* or alluded to in various chapters of *Don Quixote.* Somewhat puzzling is De Quille's reference to Don Kirieluson of Greece. *Don Quixote* speaks of a Don Belianis of Greece; the "Kyrie eleison" is a liturgical prayer in many churches.

Chapter XII.
The Cave of Mammon—"Prince Mammon"—"Son Dives" Heartily Welcomed—Mammon on the "Labor Question"—All the Metal-working Dwarfs Enslaved.

After Mr. Lemuel Gulliver left us, Dives confided to me that he was by no means at ease in mind, therefore could take no comfort in mere frivolities. He informed me that at the time he bade farewell to Earth, a former partner of his was far gone with consumption, and was liable at any time to become a passenger by old Charon's boat. He further said that this old partner had always claimed that he had wronged and ruined him; which was silly, as all was fair in business, as in love and war. Nevertheless he did not wish this man's shade to arrive at the gate of the Celestial City with his very plausible-looking story before he (Dives) had been admitted, as it might cause him some delay and annoyance.

However, Dives was willing to travel a short distance out of our direct road in order to visit the cave of Mammon. He said Plutus was a mere heathen babe, who had not a single correct idea in regard to the exigencies and requirements of modern finance, whereas Mammon was the Christian keeper and governor of wealth; besides he was a personage old in experience, as well as venerable in years.[1]

My feelings in regard to Mammon were much the same as those of Mr. Lemuel Gulliver, if I rightly interpreted his wry faces and shrugs, for I remembered that he was spoken of by Milton as—

"Mammon, the least erected spirit that fell
From Heaven: for e'en in Heaven his looks and thoughts
Were always downward bent, admiring more
The riches of Heaven's pavement, trodden gold,
Than ought divine or holy else enjoy'd
In vision beatific."[2]

We found the Cave of Mammon at the head of a deep and narrow gorge, the rock walls on each side of which were vertical and to the eye of almost unsearchable height. The gorge ended abruptly against the side of a mountain of adamantine rock, perpendicular and higher than the highest of Himalaya's peaks. Hewn out of this rock was the entrance, the doors of which were of vast bars and beams of iron and steel. Inscribed over the doors in huge letters was the motto—*"Wealth Makes the Man."*

Dives read the inscription with a smile of approval. The massive doors being closed, and no one being in sight, we were for a time in doubt as to the proper course to pursue in order to make known our arrival. However, Dives—who was now all life and activity—soon discovered suspended near by an immense gong. Seizing a large hammer that stood ready at hand, he struck the gong several heavy blows. The sounds produced resembled the pealing and crashing of thunder. Involuntarily I drew back and cast my eyes upward, fearing the whole face of the mountain would be brought down.

Soon we heard within sounds as of the falling of heavy chains, the throwing down of bars, and the grinding of keys in locks. Then one of the pair of folding doors was slightly opened, and a moment later was swung back on its hinges. Then out from the dimly lighted interior a shrill, high-pitched voice was heard to cry: "Ah, it is thee, son Dives!"

Then appeared before us in the open door a personage of a tall thin form clad in a long robe of rusty black and wearing a skull-cap of crimson velvet. The face was long and beardless, the cheeks hollow, and the high forehead filled with a thousand wrinkles, into some of which were partly sunken and knitted the strangely high and sharply arched jet black eyebrows. The eyes were not large, but were protuberant and so very sharp and black that they seemed those of a great rat. The nose was long and hooked, almost meeting the sharp and slightly upturned chin. Long, lank black hairs hung from beneath the closely-fitting cap.

At sight of this strange and striking figure, I at first feared we had aroused the wrong personage; for to me he seemed the very shape and image of Mephistopheles.

"Ah, my dear child," cried the weird being, bestowing upon Dives a sort of paternal grin, "I am glad to see thee here at last! Thou didst well in the world above—thou didst well, I must say, according to thy opportunities. For years I have longed to stand beside thee and see thee feast thy eyes upon my stores of wealth. Ah, my son, it will be to thee a rare treat—a rare treat!" and the old fellow rubbed his hands at the thought.

"While thou wert in the flesh, son Dives, I did all I could for thee, putting thee in the way of gaining many nice little nests of money; and I will say that in all things thou didst ably second me—ably second me, my son."

"I did my best, your Highness," said Dives humbly, "but that was not much."

"It was a great deal—a great deal, son Dives!" cried "Prince Mammon."

The old fellow then invited us to enter his abode, and as soon as we were within with great care put up every bar and chain, shot every bolt, and turned every key.

The hall into which we had passed was both broad and high—all hewn from solid rock. It was lighted with a few lamps ranged along the walls—lamps such, in shape, as miners use, but all of solid gold.

Taking in his hand one of the lamps, Prince Mammon made us see that the walls were almost a solid mass of gold, there being only here and there narrow ribbons of pure white quartz—"Just enough to set off the yellow metal to good advantage," said Mammon. "You see," continued the old fellow, "that like the venerable and experienced rat in the fable, I have made my nest in the very heart of the cheese," and cackling hilariously he poked Dives in the ribs with his long bony forefinger.

"It was I, son Dives, that put thee in the way of taking another than the direct road, for I wished thee to come hither; also, I wished thee to see the few gems and coins contained in the toy shop of that fool boy Plutus, before looking through my treasure-house of solid wealth.

"I have at work in the roots of this mountain chain more than five times five hundred thousand gnomes; also have employed as many dwarfs of other species, as the Getuli and Cobali, written of by Georgius Agricola,[3] and the six kinds of subterranean sprites known to Olaus Magnus.[4] These tribes of natural miners and metal-men would fain have retreated when I came hither, but obtaining the aid of an old friend of mine, and also I trust of *thine*, I was enabled to put upon them a spell that made them all mine forever—mine, fast and strong, to serve me in these precious veins to all eternity! I have no strikes in my dominions!"

"It was a master-stroke of policy to thus secure at a single move so great an army to labor in your mines," said Dives, admiringly.

"Aye, son Dives," cried Prince Mammon, exultingly—"aye, I understand the 'Labor Question'![5] And, by the way, my child, I noted with pleasure that while in the flesh thou wert of those sage souls of thy native land whose aim it was to draw upon the swarms of the Chinese Empire, even as I drew upon the swarms of the subterranean realms."[6]

"It was in order to bring the Chinese within the pale of Christian influences that I advocated their unrestricted admission into my native country," said Dives, falteringly.

"Aye, to be sure," said Mammon, with a sly wink, "it was much the same with me when I got my gnomes. The one ardent desire of my philanthropic heart was that the poor, wild rambling creatures might be brought within the benificent influences of a strong and regular form of government."

Dives smiled faintly; but said nothing.

"Your plan," continued Prince Mammon, "was almost as good as mine—was as near as you could come to it at present in your country. You see, had you been allowed to open the gates and flood the country with low-priced labor, you would at a stroke have brought all the laboring people in the land to a level with the imported class; for each low-priced laborer you brought and put into your fields, mines, and factories you would have made another at home. It was a beautiful plan—I could have thought of nothing better myself had I been there in person, as I was in spirit."

At this Dives laughed, and throwing off all disguise said: "We also gave out that we advocated the admission of the Chinese in order to promote trade with China, by keeping on the right side of the government of that country."

"I see," said Prince Mammon, "in order to be allowed to trade in China it was necessary to bring the Chinese coolie to the United States to hoe in your garden and launder your dirty linen; you meantime pumping Christian doctrine into the fellow—beautiful!"

The tone of Prince Mammon being somewhat sarcastic, Dives hastened to say: "Of course what was said in regard to the great opportunities that would be offered for the conversion of the Chinese was for the purpose of getting all the preachers on our side."

"Yes, it would have been a great thing for all the preachers," said Mammon, in a sneering tone—"it would have doubled their business. Besides all the heathen from China, there would soon have been as many of home growth. Also, your American laborers not being in a position to bring up their families in a manner to fit them to become good citizens, there would soon have been a vast deal of business for lawyers, jail-builders, and the hangman."

Dives stared at hearing this. He was too much astonished at Mammon's change of tone to utter a word.

"You see," said the old fellow, smiling, as he fixed his keen little eyes upon the confused Dives—"you see, son Dives, I am so much in love with my own system that when I begin to contemplate any other some little defects will appear. In my domain I have found the grand solution of that most troublesome of all questions, the 'Labor Question'!"

During all this time we had been passing along one side of the great hall we had at first entered, Prince Mammon halting a moment now and again to flash his lamp upon the wall, to show us that the mass of gold continued, but not interrupting the current of conversation to make any remark upon it.

Notes

1. Mammon is represented in the New Testament as the false god of wealth. Dives therefore had exactly the wrong attitude toward Mammon; he should have known that Christians are warned that they cannot serve both God and Mammon. See *Matthew* 6:24; *Luke* 16:9, 11, and 13.

2. See John Milton, *Paradise Lost*, I, 679–84.

3. Georgius Agricola (1494–1555) was Germany's earliest mineralogist. He wrote extensively on mining.

4. Olaus Magnus (1490–1558) was an eminent Swedish historian who remained loyal to Roman Catholicism and moved to Rome after Sweden became Lutheran.

5. The "labor question" of late nineteenth-century America can be briefly summarized as the problem of how to obtain laborers at a price which would afford sufficient profit to employers. Even the statement of the issue shows that the major consideration behind it was how to benefit employers. The problem had been typically addressed by immigration. Employers encouraged the immigration of cheap labor first from Europe, to work in the mills and factories of the East and Midwest, and then from the Orient, to do menial labor in the mines, railroads, and farms of the West. Westerners, however, quickly came to resent the industry and ambition of the Chinese and other Orientals—and their willingness to work for low wages—and strongly supported the discriminatory exclusion laws which, beginning in 1882, severely restricted further immigration from the Orient.

6. For a discussion of this issue, see the "Introduction," pp. 41–2, and note 61.

Chapter XIII.
Mammon's Store-House, Mint and Workshop—The Salamanders and Their Paintings—Unknown Metals.

At last we came to a chamber on one side of the hall which was lighted up by means of lamps of a large size hanging against huge pillars. These lamps, we were told, were fed by means of pipes leading from natural reservoirs of oil somewhere in the mountain, and having asbestos wicks they burned perpetually. The chamber was apparently about one thousand paces square and of immense height. Huge it was as the "many-pillared hall of the palace of Karnak."[1] The whole front was open to the great entrance hall along which we had been traveling.

As regards the appearance and contents of this chamber, I may adapt the description of Mr. Spenser, who saw it about the year 1589. He says—

> "In all that rowme was nothing to be seene
> But huge great yron chests and coffers strong,
> All bard with double bands, that no one could weene
> Them to enforce by violence or wrong;
> On every side they placed were along."[2]

We, however, saw, in addition to the "yron chests," tier upon tier of bars of pure gold of such size that in piling them up it was necessary to use traveling cranes. Against the walls in places there stood slabs of the same metal so long and broad that one of them would have served as a door for St. Paul's cathedral; and against the pillars—high as the spire of an ordinary church—these huge golden slabs were also stacked. The pillars of the great chamber were thirty paces in circumference, and we found upon inspection that all were of solid silver—unpolished and just as they were hoisted out of the mould in which they had been cast.

Seeing on all sides these massive evidences of wealth beyond the dreams of even the mightiest princes and potentates of Earth, Dives began what was intended to be an eloquent expression of his admiration of the unbounded store of wealth in the midst of which he stood. But Prince Mammon checked him almost as soon as he was fairly launched.

"Tut, tut! son Dives," said the old man, "save thy words, strength or reason and powers of comprehension. What thou here seest is a mere recess in the side of the entrance hall—I call it my lumber-room. Into it I tumble all unsightly stuff for which room cannot be found in other places and, lo! when thy unaccustomed eyes fall upon the litter of odds and ends thou thinkest it riches. Ha, ha! Why, son Dives, I fear thou wilt yet make me ashamed of thee!"

Quite crestfallen, Dives retired his enthusiasm within himself, as a turtle draws its assaulted head within its shell.

Passing out of the pillared store-house of the precious metals, and again advancing along the grand hall by which we had first entered, we presently arrived at a great brazen gate.

As we halted before the gate, Prince Mammon took up a hammer of steel and thrice struck a disk of the same metal that was fitted into the mouth of a tube which projected from one of the walls. The hammer strokes were repeated by a thousand ringing echoes—echoes that re-sounded before us, above, beneath, and on all sides, apparently in caverns and chambers of vast dimensions.

At the third stroke the gate before us receded into one of the side walls with a hollow rumble, and the instant after we had passed within it closed behind us with a crash like a peal of thunder.

The room we thus entered was of almost undiscoverable dimensions. From hundreds of spouts that projected from one of the side walls were pouring forth gold, silver, and even the bronze and copper coins, of all nations and countries.

The coins were received in cars running upon smooth steel tracks, and so quickly was each filled, whirled about and started back along the return track, that two lines or trains of the cars were kept in constant motion at carrying away the coins constantly falling in a merry, musical cascade from each broad spout. The panting, big-headed, broad-backed dwarfs whose business it was to trundle the coin-cars had hardly a moment's cessation of toil.

Overhead, above the strong vaulted ceiling, was heard a tremendous commotion of whirring, creaking, rumbling and thumping machinery. There, Prince Mammon informed us, were situated all the huge engines and coining presses.

The cars—by hundreds of tracks—conveyed the finished coins to chutes that led to vast storage vaults far below. In these was heaped a weight of wealth that would sink all the navies of the world, and then show no sign of diminution.

"I observe with some surprise," said Dives, "that you coin a deal of silver. Is it intended to circulate side by side with gold as legal tender to any amount?"

"Most assuredly, my son. It is the money of the millions of the world.

I know your thoughts, son Dives, and what you did as a representative of your people. I did not approve of it. My silver must not be made a commodity—mere merchandise. Even my copper coins are not to be despised; they are the seeds of silver and silver coins the seeds of gold."

As in his inmost soul Dives had never experienced any "sensation of cheapness" either in taking in silver or paying it out, he offered no objection to what was said by his admired master. He merely remarked that a starving man might procure that which would appease the pangs of hunger with a copper coin.

From this great chamber into which were pouring cascades of coin we were on a sudden transferred, I know not how, to an immensely deeper subterranean region. There was somewhere a sound as of an enormous gong—a sound as loud as the crash of a peal of thunder—when all was for a moment dark; and a moment after we found ourselves standing in a great room on one side of which were furnaces in long rows, all at a white heat.

Seated quite at their ease alongside the furnaces, which were filled with small pots of molten metal, were scores of copper-hued beings which Prince Mammon told us were salamanders—those creatures in human form, well known to the ancients, who are capable of dwelling in fire.[3] These wonderful beings had easels standing before them and all were busily engaged in painting. The pallets they held in their hands were red-hot, and on them they mixed the colors they were using, which colors were taken from the pots of molten metals in the furnaces. The tints were applied to the work with brushes made of asbestos or some such incombustible material.

The salamander artists were engaged in decorating all manner of wares made of the precious metals. They were also seen at work in one part of the room on large landscape pieces, sheets of metal of various kinds being used in place of canvas.

Prince Mammon informed us that the metals used as pigments were far more precious than either silver or gold, and were as yet unknown to the human race. In these metals all the primary colors were found in their full brilliancy, and also many beautiful natural tints of wonderful purity. They were all metals of greater specific gravity than any at present known to the inhabitants of Earth, and were brought up by the salamanders from depths in the region of molten metals far below the zones of silver, gold and platinum.[4] On the planet Earth, Prince Mammon said there were a few places in the Himalaya mountains, under the roots of the peaks of greatest upheaval, where some of these metals would yet be found, while on Mars and some of the other planets they were already discovered and coming into use. It was for this reason he had started his factory, as the vessels and wares made of these metals would rank in value next to diamonds and rubies.

I noted that the metals mixed on the pallets formed beautiful tints and that the work done was exquisite—far surpassing anything in enamel or in oil or water colors—while the designs were much beyond the art and imagination of the human race in this age of the earth.

Prince Mammon informed us that far beneath this work-room or atelier was a shaft that passed down through the rib or cone of an infusible rock, to the center of the planet. Down along the course of the shaft, at proper intervals, holes had been drilled out into the common or main sea of molten metals through which to draw off the kinds wanted at any particular time by means of conveniently arranged cocks.

From the upper openings were drawn off silver, gold, platinum and other such metals from their particular stratums or zones, and from lower ones the denser metals, till far below were reached those rare metals which naturally exhibited all the colors of the solar spectrum. All the work in this shaft, Prince Mammon informed us, was done by the salamanders. The gnomes, cobalds and other tribes of subterranean sprites found it too warm to work in comfort, the walls of the shaft being constantly at a white heat.

Notes

1. The temple of Karnak is a famous architectural relic. It was built by one of the Pharoahs in what was once called Thebes.

2. Edmund Spenser, *The Faerie Queene*, II, vii, 30. The stanza proceeds ominously to describe the way the room was littered with dead men's skulls and bones.

3. In ancient times, salamanders were believed capable of withstanding fire.

4. This passage reflects De Quille's knowledge of both geology and chemistry. He appears to have been familiar with Mendeleyev's Periodic Classification chart, prepared in 1869, which predicted the existence of undiscovered elements and determined their atomic weights and chief properties.

Chapter XIV.
Mammon's Little Model World—He Exults—Is Rebuked by an Angel.

Again, at a wave of the hand of Prince Mammon, came an earth-jarring sound and instantly there was darkness. In this darkness I experienced a sensation of rapid motion for a few moments, then there came a blinding light, as of the noonday sun, and we saw that we were in what appeared to be the open country. There were grassy lawns, clumps of trees and shrubs, gently rolling hills, brooks, cascades and fountains.

I was surprised and delighted. I could not refrain from saying that the beautiful country into which we had emerged was in striking contrast to the wild and savage aspect of the terrific gorge through which we had reached the entrance to the subterranean realms in which we had so long been wandering.

Prince Mammon smiled and with a sly twinkle in his eye turned to Dives, and asked what he thought of the place.

Dives declared it was the most beautiful he had ever seen.

"Did you ever see a more beautiful spot anywhere on Earth?" queried Mammon, briskly rubbing his long bony hands and gazing about the place with a smile that denoted intense satisfaction.

"Never!" cried Dives.

"How do you like the light of the sun here, is it not well tempered?"

"I find it perfect and very agreeable," said Dives, "now that my eyes have adapted themselves to it."

"I am glad to hear you say you like it," said Mammon, "for this is a little world of my own creation—a world after my own heart. It will surprise you to learn that we are still in the subterranean depths—that we are a mile or more beneath the top of the great mountain range. Pluck for me a blade or two of that fresh and dewy-looking grass, that I may show you the nature of it."

Dives moved to the edge of the broad sanded walk and vainly endeavored to pull out of the sward a single blade of the grass.

"Why," cried he, "it is like steel!"

"And it really is a metal much like steel," said Mammon, "but one infinitely more pliant and strong."

Prince Mammon next made us observe that all the brilliant flowers adorning the grounds were composed of gems of various hues, their stalks and leaves being wrought of colored metals of several kinds. The trees were also of metals, and the fruit and flowers on their boughs were of crystal and precious stones of various colors.

The brooks and fountains flowed real water, but all else seemed artificial. In the beds of the brooks all the sands were of gold, and all the pebbles were precious stones. These were of every kind known to the human race and many, of various colors and intense fire, that are not found on our planet.

The cascades tumbled down terraces of rock crystal, jet, malachite and lapis lazuli. Through these terraces ran seams of opal, turquoise, emerald and carbuncle, all so cleverly disposed as to appear to have been formed by nature. However, we found upon examination that even the patches of moss and lichens, that seemed to be overgrowing the precious stones in several places, were purely artificial—made of colored metals.

The fountains were of a kind simply indescribable as regards size, beauty of design and richness of ornamentation. So lavish had been the use of gems that through the streams of falling water were seen those of all the colors of the rainbow. From what has been said of the brooks the elaborate decoration of the fountains may be imagined.

Among the groves were groups of statuary in marble, jasper, alabaster, gold, silver and other metals to me unknown. Also there were great numbers of vases of crystal and precious metals. Many of these were several feet in height and all bore very beautiful designs wrought out in precious stones. In some groves were pagoda-like structures which so glittered with gems that they seemed exaggerated patterns of the crowns of the princes and potentates of my native planet.

It would be impossible to describe all the wealth and wonders displayed on every side in the little Mammon-made world through which we strolled during several hours; but I may say, in conclusion, that the place was not devoid of life of a certain kind, for there were thousands of singing birds of gay plumage, and animals that moved to and fro within prescribed bounds, but all were artificial—mere cunning mechanical contrivances, lacking the breath and soul of life.

Being requested by Prince Mammon to particularly observe the sun, we looked aloft and saw that which appeared to be much such a sun as illuminates our planet, but the heavens and clouds had a stiff and stagey appearance—there was a lack of depth and transparency.

After we had gazed up at the sun until well-nigh blinded, Mammon informed us that it was less than half a mile high, that it was fed by electricity drawn from the atmosphere by means not yet known to the human race, and that the great current so obtained was brought to bear upon a disk of the incombustible material in which was sunk the shaft reaching down into the molten interior of his planet.

"This," said he, waving his hand abroad, "is my pleasure-ground as well as my treasure-house. Originally it was a dark natural cave, about a mile in diameter. I have made it what you see—a pleasanter and more beautiful place than is to be found anywhere else in the whole universe. Why, the very fishes that sport in the fountains and in the pools below the falls in the brooks are artificial—all made by my cunning gnomes, as also are the humming beetles, gay butterflies, chirping crickets, and shrill cicadas!"

"All is very wonderful," said Dives.

" Now that you have seen all, son Dives, may I not boast that the griffins that dwell on the golden mountains are not so rich as I? My stores of wealth are greater far than all that are to be found in the treasure-cave of Solomon in the heart of Mount Caucasus—that cave over which the mighty Il Habul of the race of Eblis is guardian.[1] What was the Golden Palace of Nero[2], or all the wealth of Ormus and Ind[3] to a single grove, fountain or temple in this little subterranean world which I have created? What is the wealth of—?"

Even as Mammon spoke, with uplifted hand and exultant voice, his words were drowned by the shrill blast of a trumpet, and in an instant all was Cimmerian darkness. High above us, and apparently self-illuminated, then appeared the tall white-robed form of some angelic being who cried in a loud and thrilling voice: "With all thy boasted wealth and all thy power, Prince Mammon, thou canst not make one thing so good as the smile of a little child!"

Although Mammon was evidently quaking with fear, he said: "It is nothing! It is merely a silly kind of ghost that at times appears in my dominions thinking to annoy me. Yet, I like it not. Let us away!"

Notes

1. This is a puzzling allusion. Eblis is an evil spirit in Islamic mythology; hence, Solomon's fabled treasure is guarded by a demon. But Mount Caucasus is the place where Prometheus was punished for having stolen fire.

2. Nero built his Golden Palace, an edifice which severely taxed Italy and the provinces, after the fire which destroyed Rome in 64 A.D. The Palace was demolished by his opponents after his death.

3. Ormus and Ind are poetic terms for Hormuz (i.e. the Persian Gulf) and India. Both regions were synonymous with wealth.

Chapter XV.
The Terrible Shaft—Satan Arises from the Molten Sea—Mammon Tempts Dives—The Angel—Avarice and Envy.

As Mammon spoke the words—"Let us away!" there came a thunderous boom, as of a mountain rent apart. For a moment I experienced a sensation of being hurled through the air, then there came a flash of white light that was at first almost blistering to the eyeballs. We were standing beside what seemed a bottomless pit, the walls of which were at a white heat.

"This," said Mammon, pointing to the incandescent opening—"this is the shaft of which I a short time since made mention. It extends down to the molten center of the planet—down to where all the metals are fluid as water. There, in the flaming depths, at times occur convulsions and upheavals; subterranean storms that send tidal waves surging upward into all the fissures and cavities of the planet, and cause fire and flames to spout forth through those blow-holes or vents which on the planet Earth are known as volcanoes. At such times even my salamanders fear to descend into the raging regions below.

"There is only one being known to me who dares to brave the fury of the fires below when these subterranean cyclones rage. He is my friend and powerful protector. Even now he is near. I see him—I see him! He is rising—rising from the molten depths! It is not yet given you to behold him, son Dives, but the time is not distant when your eyes will know him."

Turning again to the fiery shaft and stretching forth his bony hands, Prince Mammon cried: "Ah, my noble protector! He rises—he ascends—swiftly ascends. He is here!"

Bowing profoundly, then drawing himself up, folding his arms upon his breast and gazing fixedly before him, Prince Mammon in a low and thrilling tone chanted:—

> "I see a dusk and awful figure rise,
> Like an infernal god, from out the earth;
> His face is wrapped in a mantle and his form

Robed as with angry clouds; he stands between
Thyself and me—but *I* fear him not!—"

"But I fear him, if he is a being such as you describe," cried Dives, quaking with fear—"Let us away! We are too near the region of everlasting fires—I am scorched!"

Mammon laughed until the place rang again.

"So, son Dives," said he, "you do have fears of the infernal fires? I, who know all known to any but the very highest, know that it is well that thou shouldst have misgivings. I much fear thou wilt go farther and fare worse—more I dare not tell thee. Remain with me, son Dives, and thou shalt have command next to myself in these golden caverns. Thou shalt roll in gold—shalt sleep in piles of gold with bags of diamonds for thy pillow and robes fringed with strings of pearls of the Orient for thy coverings! Here thou shalt dwell to all eternity and be safe, for my doors are always locked and double-locked with a spell known to no being but myself. What sayest thou, son Dives? Thou hast seen my wealth, wilt remain and be a partner in it—have as much use of it as I myself have?"

Dives visibly shuddered. He then began to stammer some reply, when there rang through the place the clear tones of a great bell. Instantly the incandescent shaft grew black and all was in midnight darkness. Above, in what seemed a sort of niche in the vaulted roof of the chamber, we saw the tall form of the white-robed angel and heard a voice cry:—

> "Let none admire
> That riches grow in hell: that soil may best
> Deserve the precious bane!"[1]

"Ah, the ghost again! It is the scourge and pest of my life, and beyond the reach of all spells! Let us hence!" and after a few tremendous bangings, slammings and swift rushings, as on the wings of the wind, we found ourselves set down in the dimly lighted hall before the great gate through which we first entered from the outside world.

Here Mammon again endeavored to persuade Dives to take up his abode with him, dwelling particularly upon the beauties and joys of the little world he had himself made, with a sun and all else after his own heart.

Dives was at last obliged to come out squarely. He said that, although delighted with all he had seen and the flattering manner in which he had been received, heaven was his destination and he felt it incumbent upon himself to go there and dwell among those whose good and righteous deeds on earth entitled them to the reward of a dwelling place in the Celestial City.

As Dives spoke in this strain there was a queer look about the corners of old Mammon's eyes and a queer curl of his upper lip, but he made no further attempt to induce Dives to remain. He turned to his great gate and dropping chains, drawing bolts, lifting bars, and working huge locks presently swung one of the doors open a sufficient distance to permit us to make our exit.

As we were leaving, Mammon, who stood in his narrowly opened door, called out: "Son Dives, tell St. Peter that I gave thee my blessing and heartily approved of the disposition thou didst make of thy wealth," and as he turned to secure his gate he muttered: "So I do—so I do. It will make ten thousand converts for me and my master. It was for us he worked, but the poor fool goes to another place in expectation of his reward."

I glanced at Dives, but he evidently had not heard Mammon's mutterings. His eyes were fixed upon a wild and miserable-looking wretch who occupied a hut built into one of the walls of the gorge that led to the gate of Mammon. The stones of which the hut was constructed were so stained and moss-grown that they seemed at a first glance to form a part of the cliff in a niche of which the little den was built—built as is the nest of a swallow against a wall.

The occupant of the hut was old and wrinkled—a mere mummy. He lay with head and half his length projecting from a low opening in his miserable den that did duty as a door. He was clothed in rags. He clutched a leathern purse in his left hand, supporting himself on his right, as he upreared his head from the ground. The spreading fingers of the hand upon the ground resembled the claws of a vulture. Thus stretched like a crawling savage in ambush he glared from beneath a thatch of grizzled hair at the gate which Mammon was closing. The wretch had in his eyes the hungry and desperate look of a wild beast.

As we gazed upon the miserable creature who was thus glowering at the gate of Mammon's cave, there appeared for an instant over the hut in letters of fire the word *"Avarice."*

Hardly had we taken notice of this before we heard a noise of thumping and stomping behind us. Turning we saw on the opposite side of the gorge much such a hut as that occupied by Avarice. In the little den was an old white-haired man who was peering out at Mammon's cave. As he slyly peeped out from behind his door-post, the old man ground his teeth and tore at his thin locks; then drawing back into his hut, still raging, he smote the ground with his staff. Yet, much as the sight maddened him, a moment after he was again back at the jamb of his door glaring out with inflamed eyes toward the great gate behind which lay hidden such vast store of wealth.

Over this hut flamed out the word *"Envy."*

"What beastly wretches!" cried Dives—"let us move on, the sight of the creatures sickens me."

Said I: "Prince Mammon should take the pair within his gates. They would live happily there to all eternity amid the gold and gems."

Dives halted suddenly, turned toward me and opened his lips as though about to speak, but said nothing and again moved on. I could give a pretty shrewd guess at the nature of his thoughts. He looked troubled, not to say disgusted.

Notes

1. See *Paradise Lost*, I, 690–92.

Chapter XVI.
Glimpses of the Celestial City—Dives and Judas—Dives Encourages Himself.

Without a word spoken between us, we passed down through the mighty chasm that led up to Mammon's gate. It was not until we had passed through the dusk that lay between the towering walls and moved out into the beautiful plain of the "Limbo of Myth and Fiction," where were groves, lawns, brooks, singing birds and a thousand other bright and beautiful things, that I ventured to ask Dives how he had enjoyed his visit to the palace of Prince Mammon.

"I find that we may have a surfeit of such things as Mammon treasures," answered Dives, shortly and gloomily.

As we pursued our way across the plain, I was much pleased to see walking arm in arm at no great distance genial Lemuel Gulliver and Baron Munchausen. I pointed out the pair to Dives, and proposed that we join them, but he flatly refused, saying he wanted to "get on."

Gulliver and Munchausen, who were both talking at once and sawing the air with their hands, soon passed out of sight behind a grove without having observed us, evidently to the great relief of my companion, who said: "We must loiter no more. We know nothing of time here where there is neither sun, moon nor stars; we do not know, for instance, whether we were in the cave of Mammon five hours, five days or five weeks."

"This certainly is a peculiar world," said I. "It is always day here. There is always from the golden vault above the same soft and beautiful light. It is a world surrounded with a luminous atmosphere. Undoubtedly we are upon another planet than Earth. It has all along appeared so to me, and Mammon constantly spoke of this as being a planet different from that whence we came. It must be that Charon's ferry is principally in and amid the vapors of interstellar space."

Dives seemed not to hear what I was saying, for quite abruptly he cried out: "Would to heaven we had not wandered from the straight road in that first plain! Can you anywhere see that light in the sky of which you have several times spoken?"

"It glows far before us—away beyond yonder swelling ridge," said I.

"Then let us hold our present course," said Dives, and soon he became almost as cheerful as at the time when I first met him on the plain bordering the Styx. He repeated to me the list of his bequests and ended by telling me that it was in order to found the several beneficent institutions that he had labored all his life. "My life," said he, "shows that I never had any other object in view, for I saved all for the great work. I might have foolishly squandered my wealth as others have done—frittered it away—but I kept it for the founding of noble institutions," and so he ran on until we had ascended the high ridge of which I have spoken.

Lifting our eyes we saw far before us a mount that rose across the farther bounds of a vast and verdant plain. On this mount, which seemed half a day's journey distant, we beheld a magnificent city. It stood in a blaze of golden light and reflected from its battlements, turrets, domes and spires ten thousand rays of all the hues of the rainbow. The city seemed of boundless extent. But even its domes and spires were only indistinctly seen because of the quivering brightness. It was like a city in a mirage. At one moment objects were flashed forth in all their grand outlines and the next melted away and mingled with the general brightness. From out this brightness in which the city was enshrouded there were constantly being darted upward zenith-piercing rays which wavered and swayed like the lances of light in an aurora borealis.

At the foot of the ridge on which we stood began the great rolling plain that extended to the base of the mount or plateau on which glittered the Celestial City. The plain was watered by many meandering streams and dotted with groves and clumps of many kinds of shrubbery. As we descended into it we saw groups of people in various parts. Soon we came to a broad flower-bordered path, which we conjectured might be that left-hand way which we should have taken in the beautiful region entered upon crossing the Styx.

As we descended on in the plain we were everywhere in the midst of beauties such as we had never imagined out of Eden. While slowly moving along the smooth path we had found we came upon a man of middle age seated alone under a blossoming elder-tree. Halting we asked him what place we were in. He informed us that it was there known as "Limbus Patrum,"[1] a place of rest outside of the gates of the Celestial City for certain patriarchs and others not entitled to enter the realms of the blest until the fulfillment of certain ordained events.

In this "Limbo," the man informed us, were many who existed before the time of the Redeemer. "Here dwell," said he, "many of those Israelites who murmured against Moses and were destroyed during the journey in the wilderness;[2] also Korah and his rebellious company;[3] Balaam,[4] Samson,[5] Tubal-Cain[6] and others of the Cain family, with many of the children of Israel not yet permitted to pass the gates of the Celestial

City." I asked the individual before us how long he had been a dweller in the beautiful region by which we were surrounded. "Over eighteen hundred years," said he. "Then," said I, "you will probably be able to inform us whether this place is in the interior of our old earth or is upon some other planet?"

The man smiled and said: "It is hard for us to rid ourselves of the old notions of an 'upper world' and a 'lower world,' but there is really no up nor down. Even here many still speak of our old planet Earth as the upper world and of their new home here as being in the lower world. But to answer your question, this is one of the planets or satellites of Sirius, which to your dwellers on Earth seems the greatest of the suns. Sirius, however, is not our only sun. We have four suns and from these unceasing light. There is also intense heat poured out by the suns, particularly by Sirius, but we feel little of it for the reason that we here are guarded by an envelope of vapor of great thickness which completely surrounds this planet at a certain height."

"Ah, now I understand why we have looked in vain for our old familiar sun, moon and stars," said Dives. "Why we must be a great distance from our old native planet. How could we have arrived here in so short a time?"

"Yes, the distance is great," said the old resident,—"Even light requires twenty years to go from this place to Earth, yet I can go and return in an instant. I have only to wish to be on the earth and I am there; then with the thought I am again here in this garden."

"And a beautiful place you have in this garden," said Dives. "We have nowhere seen a place to compare with this, and we have been through the treasure-house of Plutus and the cave of Mammon, where were many fine things. By the way, what do you think of silver money?"

The man frowned darkly and by the way of reply said: "A few moments ago I told you I could go to your old planet Earth and return in an instant. I have just made the trip and now I will give you the latest news. Your old partner, the man who so long suffered from consumption, is dead. He died about three hours ago and will probably be old Charon's next passenger," and at once the old resident turned his back upon Dives and took his old seat under his tree.

Dives was terribly cut up when such unexpected mention was made of the partner he had robbed—and worst of all was the news of the wronged man's death. He at once grasped my arm and pulled me away from the spot. As he did so I heard from the old settler under the tree a low chuckling laugh.

Soon after leaving this person we met a man on our path. Dives halted the traveler and pointing to the red-haired individual we had just left under the tree asked who he was. "That," said the man addressed, "that is Judas Iscariot," then added with a sneer—"I should think he would keep away from elder-trees!"[7]

As we moved on Dives said: "Now I can understand why yonder red-haired ruffian flew into such a rage when I asked him what he thought of silver money. He thought of the 'thirty pieces.' I think he lied in what he said about the death of my old partner; yet how should he know of him?" and Dives fell into a fit of musing which from the expression of his countenance was evidently not pleasant.

From bits of rising ground we presently began to obtain closer views of the Celestial City. Its domes, towers and spires became more distinct.

Dives became so enraptured with the views we caught of the shining city over the towering battlements that he quite forgot his adventure with Judas. He was delighted with the splendid appearance of all before us. Again and again he exclaimed that to gain admittance to a place so beautiful he felt himself amply repaid for all his hoarding and scheming through life. He was again well satisfied with the disposition he had made of his wealth, as he could now present himself at the gate of St. Peter with a big total to his credit in charitable deeds.

"When I stand before the gate," said he, "it will not be as a stranger. I shall be known there!"

"Ah, yes," said I with a sigh, "I have often heard and read that God is pleased with no music below so much as that heard in the thanksgiving songs of relieved widows, supported orphans and the comforted and rejoicing poor, but I have never been in a position to do more than dribble out at the spigot when I should have turned loose at the bung-hole."

"The beauty of my charity is that it has not been wasted in driblets," said Dives—"It all comes at once, like the opening of a huge reservoir, and must therefore make a great impression. In fact it comes in such shape that it cannot be overlooked and ignored."

"How happy is the lot," said I, "of one who is wafted within the gates of Heaven by the grateful prayers of the assisted poor and distressed!"

"Yes, when I found life leaving me I placed my money where it would do some such work as that," said Dives with a complacent smile.

"As for myself," said I, "I had little more to leave than would decently return my mortal tenement to the bosom of mother earth. However, I have no reason to complain of the Almighty. He always gave me plenty of wants; and wants are all that are worth living for. Woe unto the man who no longer has any wants! He is ready to be laid in the grave as useless."

Notes

1. L. "the limbo of the fathers," i.e. forefathers.
2. See, for example, *Numbers* 11, 14, and 16.
3. See *Numbers* 16.
4. See *Numbers* 22–24.
5. See *Judges* 13–16.
6. See *Genesis* 4:22.
7. The betrayal of Jesus by Judas Iscariot for thirty pieces of silver is told in *Matthew* 26–27. It is legend, however, which identifies the tree on which Judas hanged himself as an elder tree.

Chapter XVII.
The Heavenly City—St. Peter's Gate—Dives Tumbled into the Bottomless Pit—Lazarus and St. Peter.

As we walked on, and while Dives was still regaling my ears with an account of his deeds done in the flesh, we arrived at the foot of the mount or elevation on which stood the Celestial City. As we followed a broad gem-paved walk, with ascents of golden stairs leading from terrace to terrace, I saw at last—when we had attained a commanding height—that the city was not built upon a mountain, but on a plateau or great elevated plain. Upon this plain the city extended back beyond the limit of vision until at last it reached and was lost in a region where all was a sort of purple and saffron haze, but whether this was composed of aspiring mountains or a tumult of clouds I could not distinguish.

But that which most attracted my eyes and filled my mind was the Heavenly City itself, as it expanded and rose before us, dome above dome and spire upon spire, so golden and glittering that it almost caused the senses of the beholder to swoon.

"By Jove!" cried Dives, "this is grand! Why don't you know, it beats London. Here we may expect to find civilization, and here we shall be at home with the good and great of all nations!"

At the top of the last of the many flights of golden stairs lay all abroad a grand and spacious esplanade, carpeted with an emerald sward and decked with flowers of a thousand hues unknown to earth, and diffusing an odor "more sweet than Syrian unguents that flow from shells of gold." Here were sun-scattered groves and clumps of trees of kinds more stately and graceful than any of even the most favored regions of Earth. Birds like living gems peopled every bough and from whose throats tinkled forth music more sweet and soothing than even the most tuneful strains of aeolian strings. And a strange thing was that though only the gentlest of zephyrs stirred the air, the branches of the trees constantly swayed to and fro as if rocking the feathered songsters and keeping the time of their tunes.

It seemed to me that we must already be in Heaven, though we had seen neither wall nor gate.

After a long walk amid beauties such as I had never before seen even in imagination, we emerged from a sort of garden on the esplanade and found ourselves again upon the straight broad path. To our astonishment, a few steps along this path brought us to a vast and apparently bottomless gulf. Straight before us stretched a narrow causeway which seemed suspended in air. Far forth stretched the fragile bridge over the yawning and fearful abyss—an abyss filled with that which seemed neither air nor water, but "blue depth" that swayed and quivered far below. This unfathomable charm formed a broad moat about the walls of alabaster and transparent adamant, which encircled the Celestial City.

To reach this happy city the narrow causeway must be traversed. Dives—after testing the bridge by stamping upon it with all his force—shook his head and offered me the lead.

The bridge led straight across the bottomless moat and directly to a great gate of pearl, ivory, diamonds and rubies framed in gold. Upon an arch over this gate composed of a single sapphire, stood twelve shining guards from whose ever-whirling swords leaped ribbon-like flashes of living fire; and along the wall, and upon all the battlements, moved to and fro unceasingly tall tongues of flame bright as the streamers of the sun.

St. Peter stood before this glittering gate, arrayed in the unfading robes of heaven, holding in his hands the golden keys.

As we came up to the little landing on which stood the Saint Dives stepped before me and said: "St. Peter, I believe?"

Said Peter: "I am that unworthy son of Jonas so known among the sons of men."[1]

"You have no doubt heard of me," said Dives—"of Hon. Magnificus Auriferous Dives—and I desire to say that I shall esteem it as a particular favor if you will be so good as to admit with me my servant, Lysander P. Lazarus, who in his lifetime on earth, did some good, though his means have been very limited."

"Yes," said St. Peter, "we have kept an account of what Mr. Lazarus has done. There is considerable on the books to his credit."

"I am glad to hear you say so," said Dives—"It is better than I had anticipated. I suppose that with what is down to his credit, and with recommendation and influence, there will be no difficulty about letting him pass in with me?"

Seeing two of the guards on the sapphire arch halt and lean forward with scowling faces at the conclusion of Dives' speech—jets of flame leaping and hissing from the points of their swords—I was greatly abashed and not a little alarmed. Advancing half a step and bowing low, I said to St. Peter: "Your Honor, I feel that I have no claim to enter here, but should esteem it a favor, and would forever bless God, were you to permit me to cross back over the bridge and pitch my camp somewhere between the Dark River and the Golden Stairs."

"You cannot be allowed to go thither," said St. Peter—"Look, even now the way is guarded."

Looking back along the causeway I saw moving upon it an object that seemed a living thing clothed in flame.

St. Peter then turned to Dives and sternly regarding him said: "And you, sir, may I be permitted to ask upon what grounds you expect to enter here?"

Dives looked astonished, but not at all abashed, as he said: "Why, your Excellency, have you not got it down in the books that I gave millions on millions—every dollar I possessed—for the erection of many churches, several hospitals, and the founding of libraries and schools of various kinds? If all these great works are not found to be set down to my credit, I would suggest to you the propriety of discharging forthwith the present incumbent of the office of Recording Angel."

"These things are all down," said St. Peter, "but not to your credit. Do you come here in the expectation of entering into the city of Jehovah on that which but represents the sighs, groans, tears and worn out lives of the thousands of the poor and lowly among your fellowmen that you ground and oppressed in the upper world? Those tears, sighs, groans, labors and tribulations have all been set down to the credit of scores who are now within this gate, and many yet to come."

"Your Excellency, I—"

"Hold thy peace! Thou, Dives—thou hast afflicted the just; thou hast taken bribes; thou hast oppressed and walked upon God's poor; yea, and thou hast greedily gained of thy neighbor by extortion. Thou hast dealt falsely and treacherously, 'making the ephah small and the shekel great—'"[2]

"But, your Highness, my sole object—"

"No more, thou of the herds of the kine of Bashan![3] for also in thy skirts is found the blood of the innocent poor.[4] By the excellency of Jacob,[5] 'hell from beneath is moved for thee, to meet thee at thy coming.'[6] Go to thy reward with the devil and his angels!"[7]

As these last words were thundered forth, the swords of the twelve angels standing upon the sapphire arch were lowered and advanced, darting blinding fires into the eyes of Dives, and as he stepped backward, covering his face with his hands, the flaming thing I had seen guarding the causeway rushed forward. It was a monster ram whose fleece was living tongues of flame and whose horns seemed coils of red-hot steel. This creature gave Dives a mighty thwack in the rear that sent him flying into the awful abyss.

Down, down he went to where evil specters dwell within the glowing rock-ribbed gates of hell. Terrible was the shriek he uttered as he fell. "Alas, alas! poor Dives!" cried I,—"Alas, my friend and companion!" With my eyes I followed him as he went whirling downward through the blue of the bottomless deep—devils darting upon him in flocks, as eagles dart upon a tumbling and frightened fish-hawk.

Thinking that the creature I had just seen send poor Dives end over end into the bottomless pit might be fetching a compass with design to bounce me into the realms of perdition, I turned from contemplating the aerial summersaults of the death-bed friend of his race in order to observe the whereabouts of an animal so willing and capable. I found him back on guard near the center of the causeway.

"Son," said St. Peter, in a kindly tone, "I perceive that thou turnest with an air of concern to observe the movements of the creature that has just so efficiently sped thy fellow-traveler on his way. Have no fear. That which thou seest is the Holy Ram of Moriah—the ram that was sent to take the place of Isaac when Abraham, his father, would have offered him up as a sacrifice.[8] As a reward for what he suffered on that occasion he has been appointed 'Guardian of the Causeway,' and one of his duties is that thou hast but now seen him so efficiently perform."

"Your Honor," said I, "having but now seen a great philanthropist sent headlong into hell, I feel that it would be mere presumption in me to have a thought of entering the Celestial City; therefore, if I may be so bold, I would ask your Holiness to kindly call off the Holy Ram of Moriah and permit me to cross back and take up my abode in some pleasant valley of one of the limbos."

"Son, it cannot be," said St. Peter—"thou, Lysander P. Lazarus—thou art now to give an account of the deeds thou didst in the flesh. What hast thou to say to me, O Lazarus the little?"

"Your Honor," I began, my soul sinking within me—"your Honor, little of good has it been in my power to do; but I may say I have abstained from hate, and violence, from adultery, theft, fraud and avarice, and have never coveted so much as the thread of another's needle."

"But, my son, as to thy wealth—What churches and charitable institutions didst thou found with thy riches?"

"As regards wealth, your Holiness, I may truly say that I have all my life increased in riches, year by year; not through having more, but by wanting less."

"How about wine-bibbing and brawling, my son?"

"Your Honor, when in the flesh it has so happened upon occasion that I partook too freely of the cup of Bacchus, and may then have wrongfully contended with my fellow-man. However, to over-stimulate was, as your Honor knows, a fault of which the partiarch Noah was not wholly free."[9]

"It is true, my son," said St. Peter, "that on one memorable occasion Noah did exceed in wine; but he was perhaps excusable. It is to be borne in mind, my son, in extenuation of Noah's fault, that immediately before he had had a larger amount of water than had ever before or has ever since fallen to the lot of any mortal."

"Simon Peter, son of Jonas," said I, growing more confident and bold, "say nothing more of over-stimulating and I will not speak of the crowing of cocks[10]—'it is not good to make mention of ropes in the houses of the hanged.' For the same reason, if nothing be said of my little escapades in the way of fisticuffs, I will not ask who it was that cut off the right ear of Malchus, servant of the high-priest, in the garden."[11]

At this mention of the Malchus affair, St. Peter lifted his hand and stroked an embryo smile from his lips down into the tangle of his ample beard. But he soon assumed a somewhat severe look and said: "Son Lazarus, you grow bold—beware!"

Instinctively I looked behind me in order to ascertain whether the Holy Ram still kept to the center of the bridge, and as I turned again to St. Peter I caught him smuggling away another smile.

"Smile not, your Holiness," said I, "at my fear of the sheep, for when he approaches it is our stern business."

"O thou of little faith!"[12] said St. Peter, "doubtest thou that thou wouldst be buoyed up and float in safety, wert thou even launched forth into the thin air of the abyss?"

"Your Holiness," said I, "I humbly confess that I fear the experiment might prove like one we wot of wherein an attempt was made at walking upon the waters of the sea of Galilee."[13]

"Son Lazarus, cast not up to me my weakness; I had never learned to swim."

"Nor have I yet learned to fly, your Holiness," said I, then turned quickly to look for the ram. He was contentedly chewing his cud in the middle of the bridge. I then cast an eye up at the guards above the gate and found them just bringing their faces back to the form of seriousness befitting their high position.

"Let us speak no more of the past, my son; let bygones be bygones," said St. Peter. Then swinging open his gate he said: "Go right in, son Lazarus—you'll find your harp hanging upon a limb of the first big willow-tree on the right.[14] I had them get it ready for you as soon as I saw you land on the hither side of the Dark River—you'll find it all tuned up to your hand," and his Holiness took up his nightglass and began gazing down into the bottomless pit.

Notes

1. See *John* 21:15.
2. See *Amos* 8:5. The ephah was a Biblical unit of volume; the shekel a unit of weight as well as money. In other words, the seller would give less quantity than an ephah should contain, but the purchaser would have to give more weight of silver or gold than was right to balance out the illegal "shekel" weight.
3. See *Amos* 4:1. The meaning of this allusion is implied by the rest of the verse: "which oppress the poor, which crush the needy, which say to their masters, Bring, and let us drink."

4. See *Jeremiah* 2:34.

5. See *Amos* 6:8 and 8:7, and *Nahum* 2:2. In these contexts, the term "excellency of Jacob" is used ironically and angrily.

6. See *Isaiah* 14:9.

7. See *Matthew* 25:41. The rest of the verse identifies the "reward" as everlasting fire.

8. See *Genesis* 22: 1–13.

9. See *Genesis* 9:21.

10. All four of the Gospels tell how a cock crowed after Peter denied Christ.

11. See *John* 18:10.

12. See *Matthew* 14:31.

13. Lazarus mischievously reminds Peter that his reprimand, "O thou of little faith," was the same one Jesus spoke to him when he first tried to follow Jesus across the water of the sea of Galilee.

14. See *Psalm* 137:1–4. In the psalm the Jews exiled in Babylon hang their harps upon the willows because they cannot "sing the Lord's song in a strange land." De Quille subtly implies that Lazarus is now "home" again and may accompany his song of praise with one of the harps that was silenced long ago.

Chapter XVIII.
Lazarus Secures his Harp—Finds "Old Lame Jess"— The Wonders of the Menagerie.

Thanking St. Peter for his kind thoughtfulness, I marched through the gate and up the jasper and malachite-paved avenue to where I saw my harp hanging. Giving the golden strings a twang or two, I shouldered the instrument and sauntered along up to the top of a little acclivity to get a view of the place.

The shining city still seemed some distance away, but I could see the gleaming streets thereof. Bright beings were walking in the streets amid temples and palaces that shone with a thousand times the iridescent radiance of opal and mother of pearl.

I found that I was in a sort of park or garden that lay before the city. No one was in sight in any part of the grounds, yet I felt that near at hand were hovering the spirits of old-time friends from my native planet. I did not mistake. Old "Lame Jess," whom I had known in the mines of Fiddletown in fifty-two, soon materialized alongside me, with his harp on his arm.

Jess said he had been told some hours before that I was on the way. He said they always got news quite early of expected arrivals, there being a sort of aerial telegraph free to all.

"Are you an angel, Jess?" I asked.

"Of course, and a way-up one," said he.

"Then how is it that you have no wings?"

"That's all bosh about the wings. Suppose I had wings; next I would find it necessary to have a tail with which to steer my flight and a tail is a kind of adjunct I do not admire."

Thus we discoursed pleasantly together, and after we had had a long talk we plucked and ate several kinds of fruit of an ambrosial nature, light as an article of diet, but satisfying. As for drink, we sipped the nectar from the bells of beautiful flowers which spring up from that soil at the mere thought of the need of the refreshing beverages they contain.

After luncheon Jess proposed that we take a look at the museum and menagerie before going into the city, said popular institutions being at no great distance in a corner of the park. He said I need be in no hurry about going into the city, as I had all eternity before me; also, it might be well to get the hang of my harp before going up into the city to mingle with the older angels.

"Very well," said I, "there can be nothing finer in the city than the things I have already seen—that would be quite impossible."

"Ha, ha, ha!" laughed Jess—"O you innocent!" cried he—"All you have seen is as one of your alkali deserts—is as Death Valley, in comparison with the beauties in and about the city. What you have seen is merely allowed as some comfort for the miserables who dwell in the limbos and other wretched suburbs."

Jess led the way, going first to the menagerie. Upon reaching the place, the grounds pertaining to which were very extensive and well kept, I found before me an immense tank. In this tank was a huge fish. "The whale that swallowed Jonah," said Jess, waving his hand toward the big cetacean. The old fellow was sporting and spouting about the tank, apparently as well satisfied with his quarters as if he had the whole Bering Sea to flounder in. "He is the only 'blowhard' that has ever been permitted to enter these celestial realms," said Jess.

The ark of Noah, set on a little hill representing Ararat, was open to visitors. The old craft is still in a fair state of preservation, owing to the use of gopher wood in its construction. At the entrance door in the side hung a cage in which sat a dove with an olive leaf in its beak, and on the roof was perched a raven. Inside we found three tiers of compartments for animals. On a card tacked up near the entrance door were given the dimensions of the craft as follows: "Length, 525 feet; breadth, 87 feet six inches; height, 52 feet six inches." This was for the convenience of moderns.[1] "She's rather a 'Dutch-built'[2] old craft," said I. "She's not one of your ocean-greyhounds," said Jess, "but the record made by her was the best in that day, and though Captain Noah lived to be 950 years old he never saw it broken."

Next we saw Balaam's ass,[3] browsing about in a neatly enclosed lot. "Although the burro is here in the park of the city of Jehovah," said Jess, "the son of Beor, her whilom master, is still in the rural region beyond the bottomless gulf."[4]

In a shed alongside the stable of the ass was the cock that crowed when Peter denied his Master.[5] Jess told me—but I do not know how much truth there is in the story—that the reason Peter was made gate-keeper was because if they allowed him inside he "would kill the old rooster."

Passing on we came to a den containing those lions of King Darius of Babylon which refused to eat Daniel. They were six in number and of Numidian breed.[6]

"The lion will not touch the true prince,"[7] said Jess, "and Daniel was of the blood of Jehoiakim king of Judah."[8]

Hard by the den was a tent upon a platform in front of which a band of minstrels were giving a performance. "This is no comic business," said Jess; "all the songs are good and holy." It seemed to be as Jess said. I remember only the following words of the song the company were singing, and I thought it very appropriate to the place and occasion:

> "A flaming car to heaven Elias bore;
> From Pharaoh's hand was Moses saved of yore;
> Jonah escaped the whale; wild beasts grew tame
> At Daniel's feet; the youths survived the flame,
> Though bright the furnace glowed."

In this part of the grounds were many birds, beasts and creatures of various kinds which Jess said were understood to belong to Job's private collection. Here we saw the leviathan and behemoth swimming about in a special pool, while near by the unicorn, a beautiful beast, stood pawing in his stable.[9] Its body was white, the head red and the eyes blue. Its single horn, which is in the center of the forehead, is white at the base, black in the middle and red at the tip.

As great animosity exists between the unicorn and the lion, Job's specimen is stabled at a considerable distance from the den containing Daniel's lions. Spenser speaks as follows of the bad blood existing between these animals in his "Faery Queen":—

> "Like as a lyon, whose imperiall powre
> A prowd rebellious unicorn defyes."[10]

At the aviary we saw several storks and pelicans of the wilderness. Also here were kept the ravens that fed Elijah at the time when he dwelt by the brook Cherith.[11] There were two of them and they were nearly as big as ostriches.

The only statuary we saw as we strolled through this portion of the park was Lot's wife, a beautiful creation in rock-salt. Jess informed me that the salt pillar at the Dead Sea, always pointed out to travelers as Mrs. Lot, was bogus. I told him I had always taken it *cum grano salis*.[12]

Notes

1. The "convenience" Jess alludes to is the listing of the specifications in feet and inches. For the Biblical specifications in cubits see *Genesis* 6:15.

2. "Dutch-built" or "Dutch-build" was mildly pejorative slang for something heavy and ponderous.

3. See *Numbers* 22:21–33.

4. Balaam was the son of Beor. See *Numbers* 22:5. The implication is that Balaam was not yet worthy to enter the Heavenly City.

5. All four Gospels narrate this incident. For an example, see *Matthew* 26:74.

6. See *Daniel* 6:16–22. De Quille added the detail that lions came from Numidia (an ancient kingdom of northern Africa.)

7. The belief that lions would not harm a truly royal person was an old superstition. It is frequently mentioned in Renaissance literature. See, for example, *I Henry 4*, II, iv, 298–99.

8. Whether the prophet Daniel was actually related to Jehoiakim, the king of Judah, or just from the kingdom of Judah, is not clear. See *Daniel* 1:1–6.

9. The leviathan, behemoth, and unicorn are three mythical beasts mentioned in the King James Bible (see *Job* 40:15, 41:1–2, and 39:9–10, respectively.) More recent translations no longer mention "unicorn"; it is now held that a species of wild ox or buffalo was being referred to. Leviathan and behemoth were intended in the *Bible* to be understood as unique and unnatural creatures. From context in *Job* it appears that leviathan was a sea creature (not a whale) and behemoth a land, grass-eating creature. De Quille appears to have assumed that both were aquatic. His source for the description of the unicorn's horn is not the *Bible*; but there were many legendary descriptions abroad.

10. See Edmund Spenser, *The Faerie Queene*, II, 10, 1–2.

11. See *I Kings* 17:1–6. De Quille adds details, possibly to make the account more believable.

12. See *Genesis* 19:26 for the account of Lot's wife being turned into a pillar of salt. Lazarus ventures a pun with *cum grano salis*, which means "with a grain of salt."

Chapter XIX.
The Museum—Dives Seen Afloat in the Sheolean Sea—A Terrible Tumble Taken by Lazarus.

Next Jess led the way to the "Museum of Antiquities." It was ten times as large as the Crystal Palace in London, in which the world's fair of 1851 was held, as it had an area of 210 acres, as Jess informed me. It was all of gold, silver, ivory and precious stones. Its roof was formed by a single dome of rock crystal. To have examined all the relics and curiosities this vast structure contained would have required many years. I shall mention only a few of the objects to which Jess directed my attention. Among these were the seven ram's horn trumpets with which Joshua brought down the walls of Jericho;[1] the rod with which Moses smote the rock in Horeb;[2] the brazen serpent called "Nehushtan," made by Moses in the wilderness;[3] one of mother Eve's fig-leaf aprons;[4] David's sling and Goliath's spear;[5] the exhaustless cruse and meal barrel of the widow of Chereth,[6] and ten thousand other such relics of ancient times.

We saw the gallows on which Haman was hanged. It is, as reported, fifty cubits or 87 feet six inches in height;[7] so high that Mordecai could have a good view of him, even when sitting at the King's gate. There was a sheaf of barley gleaned by Ruth in the field of Boaz,[8] and one of the mandrakes that Rachel bought of Leah.[9] Near these things was a brick from the tower of Babel,[10] a bowl of manna,[11] and a lock of Absalom's hair.[12]

A great curiosity was the jawbone with which Samson slew a thousand Philistines. On the teeth of the jawbone blood stains are still to be seen, with a small stream of water flowing from a hollow place in the jaw. Alongside the jawbone of the ass are suspended the scissors with which Delilah, the Philistine trull of the valley of Sorek, cut Samson's hair.[13]

In the conservatory which is attached to the museum for the preservation of the sacred plants and trees we saw those of which mention is made in the account given of the early life of our first parents, while they were still residents of the "garden eastward in Eden."[14] Here we also found the burning bush which Moses saw at Horeb, now quite a tree. It is not a blackberry bush, but a thorn-tree, as Jess desired me to note.[15]

After going to other parts of the museum and seeing many curiosities, among which was the coat of many colors worn by Joseph at the time his brethren cast him into the pit in Dothan,[16] we returned to the open park to listen to the music of the many birds and feast our eyes with gazing upon the flowers and the beautiful trees in the places where the fountains were forever playing. There also were near the fountains, brooks and lakelets where bright insects sported among the reeds and flowering water-plants.

All these things were delightful and we long enjoyed them. At last, as we strolled along near the wall of the city, I thought of my late companion, Dives. I told Jess of his having been bounced by the "Holy Ram" and asked if he had any idea as to where he would bring up. Jess said he would fall until he reached the fiery billows of Tophet.[17] I then asked if I could not somewhere gain the top of the wall and look down into the Tartarean regions, as I would much like to see how Dives was faring.

Said Jess: "Well, yes, you might chance to see him, for it is now high tide in hell."

"High tide!" cried I—"Are there then tides in hell?"

"O yes, a regular ebb and flow every six hours of old mundane time," said Jess. "It was low tide when you crossed the causeway, otherwise you'd have seen billows of fire dashing up all about it. When the tide is out the abyss is a sort of bottomless crater—a space filled with air and as blue in its great depth as was the sky over our old planet, Earth."

"And do the fiery billows of the infernal regions surge up to near these walls from such an immeasurable depth?"

"O yes, quite up to the base of the walls on all sides of the Heavenly City; the bottomless abyss forms around the walls an impassable moat. At times of springtide the fiery spray is often dashed almost as high as the top of the wall. We may then see whole shoals of those who people the sheolean realms bobbing about in the fiery waves and rolling their swollen eyeballs up toward this holy haven of rest."

"Have you ever recognized any of our old acquaintances of the upper world?" I asked.

"O yes. I have several times had the pleasure of seeing Bob Turner—the fellow whose six-shooter gave me a game leg—buffeting the brimstone billows, while I was sitting on the top of the wall smelling at an ambrosial buttercup all wet with iced honey-dew."[18]

The tide being about at its highest, I slung my golden harp on my back and climbed a tall cocoanut-tree, pointed out to me by Jess, and got upon the wall with very little trouble.

The wall being, at the point where I landed, of polished amethyst it was very nearly as smooth as ice, but I managed to get across to the outer edge where I could look down into the sheolean gulf. The infernal billows were tossing and lashing at no great distance below. Shading my eyes from the fiery glare with my hands, I peered down and to my great surprise saw a huge iceberg lazily tumbling about just below me.

While I was marveling at this strange sight I observed that a hole had been made in the side of the iceberg, and into this hole poor Dives had been stuck as a woodpecker pegs an acorn into the bark of an oak.

My late companion appeared to be very uncomfortably situated. When he thrust his head out of his hole it roasted in the waves of fire that lashed the sides of the iceberg, and when he twisted himself about and reversed his position his brains were frozen in his skull, while his legs were smoking and sizzling in the flames.[19]

As I watched Dives thus revolving in his hole, the tide drove his floating palace quite near to the wall and I saw him roll his bloodshot eyes up to where I was seated. I waved my golden harp in the air and shouted to Dives to let him know that I had passed a successful examination. Unluckily, in my enthusiasm, I leaned too far out from the polished battlement; I toppled over and with harp and all went falling, falling and still falling into the awful bottomless abyss.

I seemed to have been falling for about nine years when I came to rest very gently and softly. As I lay thus quite at ease, except that I was so cold that the very marrow in my bones seemed to be freezing, I heard voices, and among others that of my old friend Colonel Bob. In a dreamy way I was at first much puzzled, but soon became sufficiently myself to call out and ask for help; for, as you already know, I thought I was wedged in a fissure in an iceberg. I may be doomed to remain on earth another score of years, but my belief is that my time here is short. I do not fear to enter into the other life; indeed, I long to again see and walk in the light of the bright and beautiful City of Heaven.

THE END

Notes

1. See *Joshua* 6:1–20.
2. See *Exodus* 17:1–8.
3. See *2 Kings* 18:4; also *Numbers* 21:8–9.
4. See *Genesis* 3:7.
5. See *1 Samuel* 17: 45–49.
6. See *1 Kings* 17: 8–16.
7. See *Esther* 5: 14 and 7: 10.
8. See *Ruth* 2–3.
9. See *Genesis* 30: 14–17.
10. See *Genesis* 11: 1–9.
11. See *Genesis* 16: 11–31.
12. See *2 Samuel* 18: 9–14.

13. See *Judges* 15: 14–19, and 16: 17–20. No mention is made of scissors; Delilah shaved Samson's head with a razor.

14. See *Genesis* 2:8.

15. See *Exodus* 3: 1–3. Again, De Quille adds details of his own about the "issue" of what kind of plant it might have been.

16. See *Genesis* 37: 17–36.

17. "Tophet" is used as another word for hell. It was an actual place outside of Jerusalem where human sacrifices were once made. See *Jeremiah* 19: 4.

18. This is another Dantean touch. In the *Inferno*, Dante learned that it was wrong to pity sinners whose punishment had been set by God.

19. Dante's Hell allows fire and ice to co-exist, for the greater torment of the sinners.

Appendix

Table of Textual Emendations

Two silent corrections have been made throughout: I have substituted "height" and "avarice" for De Quille's regular misspellings of "hight" and "averice." Antiquated but still recognized spellings have been left alone, as have foreign names, especially those of mythological figures which do not have a standard orthography. The middle column represents the emended text; the right-hand column, the original manuscript.

49.7	in the	it the
50.32	where	when
51.14	to be	be
51.18	to me	me
51.34	"indeed	indeed
51.37	to me	me
53.4	appears	appear
56.6	wave'"	wave?'"
57.13	Courageously	Couragiously
57.24	promontory	promantary
58.12	had	ha
58.17	mantle	mantel
59.20	"Go	Go
59.36	ferryman	ferriman
59.42	entombed	entomed
60.8	phosphorescent	phosphrescent
62.5	beautiful	beatutiful
63.2	sieve	seive
63.12	black,	black
64.14	referred	refered
64.20	set";	set;"
64.42	$500,000	$500 000
64.44	$1,000,000	$1,000 000
65.1	$250,000	$250 000
67.16	"why	why
68.24	sesame	sesami
69.7	'The	"The
69.7	Hades.'	Hades."
69.9	'That	"That

69.12	find.'"	find."
69.16	(This	[This
69.17	voice.)	voice.]
69.21	(Here	[Here
69.21	elbow.)	elbow.]
70.8	melancholy	melancholly
73.20	sphinx	sphynx
74.8	"Yes;	Yes;
74.30	were beds	beds
77.5	urgent	urgent,
77.24	contentedly,'"	contentedly,'
77.24	he,	he
78.14	lazuli	lazula
78.24	amethysts	amythists
78.26	panels	pannels
79.5	paralyzed	parylized
79.21	"No,"	"No;"
79.34	"Thou	Thou
79.41	beneficence	benificence
81.15	on earth	earth
81.18	commiserating	commisserating
82.33	contemptuous	contempuous
83.5	innocuous	inoccuous
83.43	now, do	now do,
84.24	pandemonium	pandemoneum
84.29	sieves	seives
84.31	floods	flouds
84.35	Fiddler's Green	Fiddlers Green
86.2	Bifrost	Biforst
86.6	Bifrost	Biforst
86.29	Mimir's	Mimirs
87.8	mind."	mind
90.8	Utgard-Loki	Utgard-Lok
92.16	inflicted	inflicting
93.11	streams,	streams
94.24	ragamuffins	ragmuffins
94.33	Dives.	Dives
94.35	rickety	ricketty
95.28	children	children;
96.1	land of the	land
96.19	tomb."	tomb
97.12	England'	England
97.24	were	were were
97.28	beverage	beaverage
98.13	off	of
98.33	receive.	receive:
98.35	valiant	vallient
99.9	brethren	brethern
99.17	placed	place
100.10	"Cinderella,"	"Cinderella,
100.40	dared	dare
101.8	Pantagruel,	Pantagruel

101.16	lubbers.''	lubbers.
101.25	valiant	valient
101.34	supercilious	supercillious
102.1	Pocahontas	Pocahontus
102.2	diligently	dilligently
102.8	Mammon''	Mammon
104.15	plausible-	plausable-
104.20	exigencies	exegencies
105.5	Himalaya	Himilaya
105.33	Mephistopheles	Mephistophiles
105.34	weird	wierd
106.34	Question'!	Question!'
107.19	launder	laundry
111.4	gold.''	gold.
111.11	transferred	transferrd
111.39	Himalaya	Himilaya
111.40	upheaval	upheval
111.41	indescribable	indiscribable
115.15	Caucasus	Caucases
115.24	boasted	basted
116.3	tempts	temps
116.30	and	an
116.34	mantle	mantel
120.24	''It	It
121.36	''Limbus Patrum,''	'Limbus Patrum,''
123.25	spigot	spiggot
123.39	He	he
125.26	sun-scattered	sun scattered
125.28	bough and	bough
126.10	encircled	encicled
127.18	fellowmen	fellow-
127.27	great-'''	great-''
128.9	perceive	percieve
128.18	presumption	presumtion
128.23	''Son, it	''son, it
128.39	knows, a	knows, was
129.6	garden.''	garden.
129.29	bygones	by gones
129.30	bygones	by gones
131.11	iridescent	iridiscent
131.25	that's	thats
131.27	kind of	kind
131.27	admire.''	admire.
132.17	Bering	Behring
132.31	enclosed	inclosed
132.34	gulf.''	gulf.
132.43	Numidian	Numidean
133.2	business,''	business;''
133.3	Jess;	Jess,
133.13	behemoth	behemath
135.8	Its	It
136.5	gazing	gazzing
136.6	fountains,	fountains